THE PRESENCE OF

WALT WHITMAN

THE PRESENCE OF WALT WHITMAN

Selected Papers from the English Institute

Edited with a Foreword by R. W. B. Lewis

COLUMBIA UNIVERSITY PRESS

New York and London

The drawings are by Angela Conner

Copyright © 1962 Columbia University Press

First printing 1962
Second printing 1965

Library of Congress Catalog Card Number 62-18255

Printed in the United States of America

To the Memory of
Stephen Emerson Whicher
1915–1961

The first four essays in this volume were delivered at the English Institute in September, 1960, in a series, organized by the editor, on Whitman's "Out of the Cradle Endlessly Rocking"; the reader's attention is drawn to the different versions of that poem that appear at the back of this book. The remaining three essays formed part of a second series, planned in some degree as a sequel to the first and given in September, 1961, under the chairmanship of Professor Lewis Leary.

The aim of the two groups combined was to offer an appraisal of Whitman's poetry and of his place in modern letters which, among other things, would bring to bear the variety of recent studies, here and abroad, whereby a "revolution in taste" regarding Whitman has been going forward—and, in a sense, to signal the end of that revolution. The aim, also, was to test a characteristic and major achievement of Whitman by taking a number of close looks at it in differing perspectives; and to reflect upon the successive phases of his career and his complex relation to his own literary generation and to some aspects of twentieth-century writing. The volume that resulted does, I think, testify to the remarkable and continuing *presence* of Walt Whitman, despite persistent efforts in certain learned and fashionable quarters over many years to belittle or simply to neglect him. No American poet has been remonstrated with so frequently; but no body of poetry has continued so firmly and obstinately to exert and to renew its power and its invigorating influence on readers and poets across several continents. It is the intention of the present contributors to determine the source and nature of that power, and to separate it out from other dimensions and masks of Whitman that have also, not only persisted, but till recently prevailed.

Whitman's poetry, indeed, tends to rouse its critics to remonstrating with each other, as this volume also suggests. Disagreements about the man and his career turn up on many pages here; and although they are expressed with all courtesy, they come with such force of concern that one is tempted to adapt Melville's spirited question to Hawthorne about metaphysics and ask, "What's the reason that in the last stages of Whitman criticism a fellow always falls to *swearing* so?" The reason in the present case, no doubt, is the enormous importance of Whitman, an importance at once profound and immediate and one that somehow is never felt without a sense of astonishment and of urgency. A view of Whitman—so these essays indicate—participates necessarily in a view of tragedy and comedy, of artistic form, of the function and responsibility of the poet, of the peculiar energies of language, of the shaping qualities and major traditions of American and European literature. It seems not too much to say that it participates in one's view of first causes and last things, of life and of death.

Mr. Chase, for example, while honoring "Out of the Cradle" highly, refuses to rank it among the world's greatest poems and places it below Whitman's own "Song of Myself" and "The Sleepers," on the grounds that it fails to reach the tragic statement it seems to be aiming at. Mr. Whicher, on the other hand, sees it (with one or two other poems of the same period) as the peak of Whitman's achievement, exactly because it *is* tragic: a tragedy of the Reason, as he calls it, and one that enacts the most traditional and Shakespearean kind of tragic acceptance. Mr. Fussell finds the same poem fulfilling itself superbly in a mode of psychological and aesthetic reconciliation; Mr. Chase, again, deprecates the poem's conclusion as unearned and argues that reconciliation in any mode is something American writers (by all means including Whitman) have at their best staunchly held back from. Mr. Pearce, meanwhile, is willing to argue not only that the 1860 edition of *Leaves of Grass* embodies the great and authentic Whitman but that the editions of 1855 and 1856 should be regarded essentially as steps en route to 1860—a judgment probably no one of the other commentators (certainly not Mr. Wright) would accept without reservation. Most of the latter, however, would evidently join with Mr. Pearce in debating with Mr. Miller the merits of Whitman's poetry after 1867 ("Passage to India" and others) and of the bardic and prophetic impulses of Whitman toward which Mr. Miller appears somewhat more hospitable than they. Again, Mr. Pearce (like Charles Feidelson, in *Symbolism and American Literature*) locates Whitman in that poetic development that extends from Romanticism through symbolism and reaches its American culmination in Wallace Stevens: the development, let us say, that identifies poetry as primarily a matter of language, of the mysterious powers that language secretes and can release; and that identifies the creative process itself, along with the relation between the artist and his materials, as the genuine subject of poetry and the supreme paradigm for any other subject that poetry may pretend to confront. Mr. Hynes, while acknowledging Whitman's significant relation to that tradition (a relation, incidentally, scarcely acknowledged before the present decade by anybody *except* Wallace Stevens), contends that in many ways Whitman is still more closely related to the counterdevelopment that extends through Pound to Williams and that pins its faith not in words or ideas but in things, whereby not the creative act but the palpable content of the world is poetry's subject and its justification. And so on.

These stimulating disagreements bespeak the multitudinous largeness, the fertile contrariety, that Whitman liked to claim for himself; and they are convincing evidence that Whitman succeeded artistically in just the way he hoped to succeed. "I round and finish little," he said in "A Backward Glance O'er Travel'd Roads" (1888). "The reader will always have his or her part to do, just as much as I have had mine." About Whitman's poetry there is a subtle question of metaphysical status, its precise mode and place of existence; but if there can be such a thing (it is arguable) as a democratic metaphysic, such was Whitman's— for his poetry really exists somewhere between the creative impulse that went into it and the reactive impulse that comes out of any individual reader. Each of the critics in this volume, consequently, has had his part to do in the making of Whitman's poetry; and each, quite properly, has rounded and finished a Whitman who is inevitably different, in greater or lesser degree, from that of any other. Mr. Chase quotes Leslie Fiedler as referring to *"Our* Whitman"; but after attending to the qualities of "our Whitman," this editor confesses that he makes out in that figure only Mr. Fiedler's Whitman—though that is, to be sure, a figure that contains many qualities in common with the editor's Whitman.

Still, surrounding these differences of judgment and emphasis, there is a remarkably large area of concurrence and coherence of attitude. Whitman emerges from the essays that follow not as a good gray bard, not as cheerleader for democracy or a prophet of cosmic unity—but as one of the great masters of poetry in English. He appears here as a poet who was no more wild and untutored than Shakespeare; who warrants examination by every critical instrument we possess; and the range of whose influence and affinities is almost immeasurable. His prosody responds to the exacting analysis of Mr. Fussell and Mr. Wright, and his language to that of Mr. Pearce and Mr. Miller. Mr. Whicher, in his characteristically searching and prehensile way, discloses in Whitman's poetic career up to 1860 a "voyage of the mind" almost as strenuous and "athletic" and always as dangerous as that of Melville; yet a voyage that announced itself in a habitual and personal idiom that for long concealed its own sometimes fearsome nature. We are reminded meanwhile of Whitman's exceedingly perceptive appreciation of his contemporaries—Longfellow and Poe, for example. Whitman had a more sophisticated and far more magnanimous understanding of the technically conservative American poets (we might add the name of Bryant) than many of his later admirers, who often have to demolish somebody else in order to celebrate Whitman; and Whitman's remarks about those contemporaries—Mr. Wright makes a large point about this—reveal how astonishingly clear and essentially modest was his awareness of his own artistic innovations. Beyond that, Mr. Fussell and Mr. Chase in particular draw telling parallels between the structures of Whitman's poems and the structures of certain American *novels*. Mr. Miller explores a major instance (Dylan Thomas) of Whitman's nutritive power abroad, and while doing so joins Mr. Chase in insisting upon the crucial and enduring element of comedy in Whitman's language and his spirit. Mr. Wright adduces Whitman's importance for several Spanish poets and traces the American influence beyond Wallace Stevens to the latest compositions of Louis Simpson, Denise Levertov, and Robert Bly. Such findings add support to Mr. Pearce's claim— huge in scope but nicely modified in statement—that Whitman participated in the very "invention" of modern poetry. To judge from these essays, anyhow (I am not sure whether this is a larger or a smaller claim), Whitman's poetry—more than the work of any other single writer—provides a synecdoche for the whole of American literature.

In all of this, of course, we may be running a very great risk— the risk of so firmly identifying Whitman and so establishing him in a network of literary relationships and inside various familiar traditions that we lose forever the startlingly original, the emotionally and intellectually unpredictable, the antic and disturbing and fascinatingly ambivalent poet our sense of whom led to the present critical effort in the first place. I have said that these essays perhaps conclude a "revolution in taste"—and in understanding—with regard to Whitman. But the process of any revolution is always more exciting and may be closer to the truth of the issue in question than is the victory at last achieved: especially since victory is notoriously other than, sometimes opposite to, the one aimed at during the struggle. The present volume, I should like to think, manages to avoid impaling on either horn of the dilemma. In demonstrating that Whitman's poetry can be investigated with the same kind of meticulous care we are used to bringing, say, to "The Waste Land" or "The Canonization" or "The Rape of the Lock"; in comparing Whitman's metaphysical tussling with that of Melville; in relating Whitman to American romance-novelists and to later American and European poets; these critics are setting forth the terms both of Whitman's accomplishment *and* of his uniqueness. They have given us, perhaps, an illustration of Northrop Frye's theory: that the *poetry* of any given poem comes out of poetry itself; but the content, attitude, and inflection come directly from the poet's unique psyche.

Those, finally, are the two elements in Whitman that the volume seems most concerned with. Whitman, that is to say, comes to us here as a Poet and as a Self; he comes to us, indeed, as the Poet *of* the Self, and of one of the most extraordinary selves since Montaigne. In these pages, Whitman is a poet in the sense of being just that rather than a number of other things he has been alleged to be—a spokesman, or a prophet, or (worse yet, as Mr. Wright emphasizes) a sanction for coarseness of spirit and slovenliness of craft. This Whitman is a maker of what he called "pomes"; and he made them the way great poets have always made poems—out of poetry. But he was also a self, recording in his characteristic rising and falling rhythms and his own incomparable play and twist of language the story of that self: of its response to an overwhelming sense of life and an immense consciousness of death, to an impulse toward expansion and an impulse toward annihilation, to an irresistible comic urge and a deeply tragic insight, to a passion for utter truth and honesty and a temptation to conceal and evade. The relation between that self and the external *world* of persons and places and things would have come more clearly into view if the particular poem chosen had been, for example, "Crossing Brooklyn Ferry"; and the paradoxes of Whitman's relation to America would have been illuminated by an essay on *Democratic Vistas*. There is much more yet to round and finish. But these discussions, I dare hope, focus on what is properly the first object of focus with respect to Whitman—on the poet and the self, and the century-long and endlessly seminal interaction between them.

The essays by Stephen E. Whicher and Roy Harvey Pearce previously appeared in *Studies in Romanticism* and the *Minnesota Review,* respectively, and are reprinted here by permission of those journals. Acknowledgment is also made to Wesleyan University Press for permission to quote the poem "Walt Whitman in the Civil War Hospitals" from *Say Pardon* by David Ignatow (copyright © 1957 by David Ignatow) and to New Directions for permission to quote from the following works: Dylan Thomas, *Collected Poems* (copyright 1939, © 1957 by New Directions); Dylan Thomas, *Letters to Vernon Watkins,* edited by Vernon Watkins (copyright © 1957 by New Directions); Ezra Pound, *Personae* (copyright 1926, 1954 by Ezra Pound); and Ezra Pound, *The Cantos* (copyright 1934, 1948 by Ezra Pound). The poem by Robert Bly, "After the Industrial Revolution, All Things Happen at Once," is quoted by permission of the author.

R. W. B. LEWIS

Yale University
February, 1962

CONTENTS

vii FOREWORD
     R. W. B. Lewis

1 WHITMAN'S AWAKENING TO DEATH: TOWARD A BIOGRAPHICAL
    READING OF "OUT OF THE CRADLE ENDLESSLY ROCKING"
    Stephen E. Whicher

28 WHITMAN'S CURIOUS WARBLE: REMINISCENCE AND
    RECONCILIATION
    Paul Fussell, Jr.

52 "OUT OF THE CRADLE" AS A ROMANCE
    Richard Chase

72 WHITMAN JUSTIFIED: THE POET IN 1860
    Roy Harvey Pearce

110 WHITMAN, POUND, AND THE PROSE TRADITION
    Samuel Hynes

137 WHITMAN AND THOMAS: THE YAWP AND THE GAB
    James E. Miller, Jr.

164 THE DELICACY OF WALT WHITMAN
    James A. Wright

190   APPENDIX: VERSIONS OF "OUT OF THE CRADLE ENDLESSLY
        ROCKING"

207   BIBLIOGRAPHY OF WORKS CITED

208   SUPERVISING COMMITTEE, 1961

209   PROGRAM

211   REGISTRANTS

THE PRESENCE OF

WALT WHITMAN

Stephen E. Whicher

WHITMAN'S AWAKENING TO DEATH

Toward a Biographical Reading of "Out of the Cradle Endlessly Rocking"

There is no life in thee, now, except that rocking life imparted by a gently rolling ship; by her, borrowed from the sea; by the sea, from the inscrutable tides of God. But while this sleep, this dream is on ye, move your foot or hand an inch; slip your hold at all; and your identity comes back in horror. Over Descartian vortices you hover. And perhaps, at mid-day, in the fairest weather, with one half-throttled shriek you drop through that transparent air into the summer sea, no more to rise for ever. Heed it well, ye Pantheists!

Moby-Dick, "The Masthead"

It is still too little realized that, with the possible but not obvious exception of Melville, no American author has ever engaged in a more daring or eventful voyage of the mind than Whitman. In his later years Whitman himself for some reason attempted to hide its extent, retouched and toned down his most revealing poems and ingeniously fitted them together into a structure toward which he claimed he had been working all the time. This jerry-built monument to the aging Whitman, which remains to this day the basis of nearly all anthologies of his work and is still reverently toured by uncritical guides, is actually a major obstacle to the recognition of his true stature. Fortunately a strong critical tradition [1] has now for many years been working to lay bare for us the real structure of Whitman's work, the spiritual biography that emerges from a comparative reading of all the editions of his *Leaves of Grass*. In this paper I wish to reexamine some part of this story as it emerges from certain key poems of the 1855 and 1860 editions, in particular "Out of the Cradle."

For this purpose it is convenient to accept the periods, or phases, which Floyd Stovall distinguished nearly thirty years ago and which time has only confirmed (the names are mine): Whitman's first or transcendental phase runs from 1855 through 1858; the second or tragic phase begins with 1859 and runs through the first publication of "When Lilacs Last" in 1865; the third or philosophic phase comprises the rest of his poetic career. This is the framework of the discussion that follows, which will center on the years 1855-60. In these years, I shall argue, it is not enough to say that a new note entered Whitman's work or that he passed through a time of serious trouble; the whole character of his work was radically and permanently altered. To trace this change in

[1] See particularly Catel, Schyberg, and Asselineau (see bibliography). This paper starts from their essential conclusions and attempts to take a further step. In particular, it accepts without argument Schyberg's conjecture of an emotional crisis between 1857 and 1860 and of some sort of homosexual "love affair" to explain it, and uses this assumption as a basis for the interpretation of some of the poems from which it was first conjectured. For the resulting hypothesis, sometimes for convenience stated at if it were fact, I ask only the minimum privilege of any such construction, a willing suspension of disbelief for long enough to make the statement possible. For convenience also, I write often as if the actual Whitman and the speaker in his poems were one and the same. Though I hope I may be permitted such shorthand devices in this brief paper, a full statement of these matters should of course constantly remind us that we are charting the drift of a highly active imagination, not reconstructing actual events.

the space I have I will focus on one theme only, what Asselineau calls Whitman's obsession with death.

A major theme of the poems of the first phase, of course, is the poet's victory over death. In every possible way these poems deny the finality of death and proclaim immortality. In this they make particularly plain what Schyberg has called Whitman's "optimism in defiance," for a preoccupation with death marks not merely the young Whitman's Emmeline Grangerford period but later apprentice work, too, and is evidenced in the early *Leaves* themselves in the very frequency with which his victory has to be reenacted. The thought of death was clearly the chief threat his vision had to overcome. It did so not by doctrine nor any merely conceptual means but by lifting him to a Life that in its own nature contradicted death. He was relieved of his fear of death by becoming one with a life-force to which death simply *was not*.

The logic of his position is stated by Emerson, whose service to the reader of Whitman is often to give conceptual definition to attitudes and insights which are too close to Whitman for definition, which he does not state because he lives them. Immortality, for Emerson, has nothing to do with duration or continuance. Rather it is "an intellectual quality," or even "an energy."

> He has it, and he alone, who gives life to all names, persons, things, where he comes. No religion, not the wildest mythology dies for him; no art is lost. He vivifies what he touches. Future state is an illusion for the ever-present state. It is not length of life, but depth of life. It is not duration, but a taking of the soul out of time, as all high action of the mind does: when we are living in the sentiments we ask no questions

about time. The spiritual world takes place;—that which is always the same.[2]

Is this not equally the position of Whitman, whom Emerson might as well have been describing in this passage? In those first years Whitman could merge with an energy to which death was an irrelevance.

Of course we must translate a bit. Emerson's concept of a qualitative immortality is essentially ethical, a neo-stoicism, while Whitman's experience of it is an instinctive release of soul that carries no particular ethical condition except that one be capable of achieving it. One consequence is that the Life Whitman enters encompasses all time but is not out of time altogether, as is Emerson's. Lifted on its flood Whitman acquires a cosmic memory and a godlike prevision and can move backward and forward at will through the remotest ages. Unlike Emerson's Over-Soul, for which history is biography, the biography of Whitman's "Me myself" is history, but it is equally deathless since it is the life-force itself. Essentially, it brings him the same assurance, an ever-present Life beside which death is simply unreal.

Yet the force of this kind of transcendental vision derives partly from the fact that it *is* vision; Whitman holds to it so strongly because he is also aware that in his actual existence he continues to hover over the universal plunge into annihilation. Man's vision can transcend his mortal condition but cannot change it. Emerson confronted this fact and confessed he had nothing very helpful to say about it. "The event of death is always astounding, our philosophy never reaches, never possesses it; we are always at the

[2] "Immortality," *Letters and Social Aims,* in *Complete Works,* Centenary Edition (Boston and New York, 1904), VIII, 347.

beginning of our catechism; always the definition is yet to be made." The best he could do was to repeat his ethical talisman, "Think on living." "Simply I have nothing to do" with "that question of another life." Whitman, I would say, takes the same position but because of the existential mode in which he writes can defend it more powerfully, if also more confusingly.

In Emerson's terms, it is the Reason that sees the ever-present immortality while the Understanding can see only the event of death. Both are right, but the poet by a fable can entice the Understanding out of its fears and so, as Plato put it, charm the child in the soul. This is the true function of those suggestions of a future state that certainly are to be found everywhere in these poems. Does Whitman, for example, believe in metempsychosis, as is so often asserted? It is hard to deny it, yet I would suggest that such a statement of the matter misses the point. These hints and guesses are bits of fable, *mythos,* "as-if" fragments scattered on the waters for the Understanding to cling to and support its unbelief. They are preparatory, instrumental, "indirect," intended not to assert anything directly but to throw the mind into the proper attitude to move beyond their metaphoric suggestions into the inwardness of pure truth. When Whitman exclaims of the dead, for example, "They are alive and well somewhere," his intention is not to tell us some fact but to stir us to feel about the dead *as if* that were the fact. All these hints of belief in the future that are thrown off from the first-phase poems, like sparkles from a pinwheel, are best taken as a measure of Whitman's confidence, exuberant enactments of the power and endless life which is his *now*. Essentially the faith from which they spring is self-sustaining and needs no doctrine to prop it; as Emerson said, the faith is the evidence. Life is; death is not: that is all Whitman knows or needs to know.

Such faith by inspection has the advantage that it is not tied to any formula and is not refutable by an argument. Its disadvantage is that it tends to die with the inspiration that brings it. The visionary gleam comes and goes by laws of its own, and each time it goes it leaves its votary face to face with the same spiritual emergency. It is not simply that the vision dies and is replaced by the unaltered facts it had denied. Vision itself is treacherous. A man may "loafe and invite" his soul but he cannot predict or control what will accept the invitation. Vision may be demonic as well as transcendental, a nightmare confirmation of dread instead of a release of power and hope.

Both modes of vision are strong in Whitman from the beginning of his work; the stronger the poem, the more its dynamics are controlled by the battle between the two. In the 1855 poems the transcendental mode is dominant and the demonic recessive, but its concealed strength is great. It shows its teeth everywhere in "Song of Myself," something like one-fifteenth of the whole being of this character. More significant than its amount is its position. It touches with its threat the key passage on the meaning of the grass; it creeps in intermittently to darken the catalogues; and in the central sections it seizes control of the poem altogether and hammers at the poet with image after image of agony and defeat ("O Christ! My fit is mastering me!") until, cuffed and stunned, he wins a moment's respite and in that interval the transcendental vision sweeps back "replenished with supreme power." Even at the end, though no longer with power to alarm, a breath of nightmare returns and the poet must reconfirm his victory:

Of the turbid pool that lies in the autumn forest,
Of the moon that descends the steeps of the soughing twilight,
Toss, sparkles of day and dusk. . . . toss on the black stems
  that decay in the muck,
Toss to the moaning gibberish of the dry limbs.

I ascend from the moon . . . . I ascend from the night,
And perceive of the ghastly glitter the sunbeams reflected,
And debouch to the steady and central from the offspring
  great or small.[3]

This dark element in the poem is by no means incidental; it is
the enemy the hero exists to fight. "Song of Myself" is the epic of
his victory. As with all Titanic heroes, as with the angels in
Paradise Lost, his struggle is a bit unconvincing since we cannot
really believe in the possibility of his defeat. But this appearance
of invincibility is the true illusion, not the threat to it. That is
supported not merely by the worldly trippers and askers around
him but by the voices of doubt within him, "saying/ That this
was all folly." The hero's victory is earned; his power is needed;
his air of omnipotence is the euphoria of a danger overcome.

[3] All quotations in this paper are from the earliest published version of
the poem cited: the 1855 version of "Song of Myself" and "The Sleepers,"
the 1860 version of "As I Ebb'd," that of the MS version of "Scented
Herbage," and for "Out of the Cradle," the poem entitled "A Child's
Reminiscence" which was published in the *Saturday Press* for December
27, 1859, and republished by Thomas O. Mabbott and Rollo G. Silver,
University of Washington Quartos, No. 1 (Seattle, 1930). For clarity, however, I use the final titles. I have tried to read these poems without pre-
conceptions imported from the more familiar revised versions, and I must
ask anyone who would examine my conclusions to do the same.

If "Song of Myself" did not in itself tell us this, as it does, another poem of the 1855 edition makes it plain, the great companion piece to "Song of Myself" which Whitman eventually called "The Sleepers." That this poem also, like the other poems of this volume, brings us to the security which they were all written to celebrate should not prevent us from seeing that it does so by a very different road. The first line, "I wander all night with my vision," sounds like the start of a section of "Song of Myself," but we quickly see that this is not the same "I" nor the same vision: "Wandering and confused . . . . lost to myself . . . . ill-assorted . . . . contradictory." This "I" is not "Myself" but is "lost to myself." It is a night consciousness, troubled, confused, disembodied, will-less and disorganized like the mind in sleep. The expansive energy of "Song of Myself" is withdrawn from this poem; the speaker here is passive and powerless. He is therefore *exposed* in a way the hero of "Song of Myself" was not. He encounters at once images of death and defeat—

> The wretched features of ennuyees, the white features of corpses, the livid faces of drunkards, the sick-gray faces of onanists,
> The gashed bodies on battlefields, the insane in their strong-doored rooms, the sacred idiots. . . .

Eighteen of the twenty-five classes of sleeper specified in the first twenty-six lines of the poem are disturbing in some way, samples of evil, distress, or death. The center of this poem, we soon see, is not life but death. The chief sleeper is the transcendental assurance of life that controls "Song of Myself." That poem had said, not without a struggle, "The dead are not dead." "The Sleepers"

says, "Here they lie." Quite deliberately, I think, Whitman here
permits to speak the darker under-consciousness which his waking vision had put down but which remained and must remain
part of his truth.

The chief evidence for this conclusion is the long section of the
poem, following the introductory description of the sleepers as
they lie "stretched and still," in which the poet somnambulistically
enters and becomes a succession of dreams. Though the fiction
of this section is that these are a miscellaneous sample of the
dreams of a number of people, we cannot get very far into it without realizing that they look more like the dreams of one consciousness. Certain points can be made about them: (1) They are
connected by numerous ties of detail, action, and mood and can
be made with little forcing to tell a continuous story, a story
which, as is appropriate to the unconscious autobiography that
emerges in such dreams, is essentially an oedipal one. (2) Their
dominant mood is one of anxiety and guilt; one after another
they present images of disaster and loss. Even when the poet makes
a visible effort to extricate himself from their oppression it continues to control him, modulating at last into the murderous
anger that is concomitant with such feelings. (3) Certain of the
individual dreams seem to offer a deliberate contrast to "Song of
Myself." During the sermon that concludes "Song of Myself,"
for example, the prophet-god says to his disciple,

> Long have you timidly waded, holding a plank by the shore,
> Now I will you to be a bold swimmer,
> To jump off in the midst of the sea, and rise again and nod
>   to me and shout, and laughingly dash with your hair.

Now this bold swimmer returns, only to be dashed on the rocks and killed, while the dreamer watches helplessly from the shore. And a few lines earlier, when the dreamer has become a shroud to wrap a body in the grave, the grave does not "multiply what has been confided" to it, nor does the corpse rise.

> It seems to me that everything in the light and air ought to
>   be happy;
> Whoever is not in his coffin and the dark grave, let him know
>   he has enough.

In this part of the poem Whitman does not merely return to the thought of death but reveals through these dreams some of the reasons for his preoccupation with it. He taps a part of the something-settled matter in his heart whose threat permanently underlay his transcendental vision. The great upsurge of creative activity, Catel points out, which produced the 1855 *Leaves of Grass* partially resolved the conflicts that led to it, but only partially, "for the work of art, even if a substitute for action, does not exhaust the forces that lie in a dream-filled sleep within us" (p. 8). In "The Sleepers" these forces stir.

I must not leave this poem, however, without noting the chief fact about it, namely that these dreams *are* dreams. Their content, which I am suggesting is as real as anything in Whitman, can reach such full expression only because it does so in the guise of dreams, just as the theme of death can enter this poem with so little resistance because these dead are not dead, but sleepers merely. I have been stressing one element of the consciousness that controls this poem because it comes closest to the dark or demonic underside of Whitman's vision which I am concerned to bring out, but there is another element, strong from the beginning, which takes over after the dream sequence is over and erases its anxieties in an all-embracing consolation. This might be called the maternal element, the thought of sleep not as death or self-loss but as rest and restoration. Here certainly one cannot maintain that Whitman does not assert a belief in the future, for the poem rests for its consolation entirely on the analogy of death and night. As sleep banishes the cares that infest the day, so the dead "pass the invigoration of the night and the chemistry of the night and awake" to new life. I will not try to worry Whitman's beautiful fable into consistency with my general position, though I think it could be done, but simply note that this night-myth of restoration, like the day-myth of an unwounded wholeness that needs no restoration, is a total one. Both combine with all of the 1855 poems to celebrate life's perfection.

II

The poems of 1856 and the poems in the Valentine MSS which Bowers dates 1857 do not evidence any basic change of position. Whitman continues to affirm life and immortality, proclaims the perfection of nature, including the body and all its functions, announces his perfect happiness, and begins a systematic program of applying his affirmative insight to every aspect of the world around him. A few poems of 1857, however, strike a darker note. "I Sit and Look Out" is among this number, as are "A Hand-Mirror," "Confession and Warning," "Of Him I Love Day and Night," and one or two more. Thoughts of guilt, evil, and death emerge in these short lyrics without any compensating affirmation except the context of other poems. We notice also that a largely 1857 poem of affirmation like "A Song of Joys" is in places more wildly exuberant, more desperately aggressive in tone than anything that had preceded it. These and other small indications suggest that the wave of confidence that crested in 1855 is beginning to falter and break of its own momentum. The blow that apparently struck the man in 1858 or 1859 precipitated a crisis in his poems and no doubt deepened it, but some crisis or other was bound to occur in any case.

For some reason, perhaps simply that Whitman was busy, no poems can be certainly dated 1858. The year 1859 was the Calamus year. Of the twenty-six poems in the Valentine MSS that were probably written in 1859, twenty-two are Calamus poems, whereas almost none that can be dated earlier are clearly of this kind. The "Calamus fragrance," to use Bowers's expression, that sifts into the two program poems of the 1860 edition, "Starting from Paumanok" and "So Long," was apparently added in 1959. Add the half a dozen or so more Calamus poems that appeared in the 1860 edition, all of which may well date from 1859 also, and you have just about all the Calamus material in *Leaves of Grass.* In 1859, give or take a few months, Whitman wrote nearly all the Calamus poems he was to write and wrote little else. In view of these facts, his later contention that these poems were part of a considered program toward which he was moving from the beginning seems highly unlikely. Rather, something utterly unforeseen has irrupted into his work, sweeping the rest of it aside and engrossing both man and poet. What the source of this new thing was can be conjectured, though we do not know the biographical facts. Whitman had some sort of unhappy love relation with a man, one that brought him a brief glimpse of happiness and then plunged him into bitter suffering. His suffering, we may believe, was intensified by the confirmation of his darkest suspicions about his own nature. To someone who, like his time and place, was in many ways as unsophisticated and even puritanical in sexual matters as Whitman seems to have been, for all his big talk, this decisive demonstration of his own difference came as a bewildering shock.

The consequences for his poetry of this crisis are spelled out for us in one of the three "summation" poems that came out of this year, "As I Ebb'd with the Ocean of Life," [4] which reads like a conscious repudiation of "Song of Myself." The central figure is the poet—and in early notebook drafts, as well as in the Preface, the hero of the 1855 edition was the poet—engaged in the same search for "types" from which he had once gathered such a rich harvest. Nature ironically offers him the trash on the water's edge, and with a shock of recognition he finds in it the emblem of his present state, namely his inability any more to see saving emblems. The poem is a farewell to his poetic vocation—premature, as it turned out, but nonetheless deeply sincere at the time. Instead of a "liberating god" and his triumphant songs of celebration, he and his "arrogant poems" are nothing, "debris." The "real Me" he thought he had courted and won in "Song of Myself" "still stands untouched, untold, altogether unreached." Instead, he is "held by

[4] The other two being "Scented Herbage of My Breast" and "Out of the Cradle." The order in which I discuss these poems is the one that best fits my argument. Actually, "As I Ebb'd" was quite possibly written last, at a time when, as in "Out of the Cradle," Whitman had reached enough perspective on his crisis to permit him to treat it in poetry. The ebb and flow of the emotional life does not follow the tidy patterns that are necessary for its exposition.

the eternal self of me that threatens to get the better of me, and stifle me." He and the "Me myself" are opposed, not in union; in Melville's words, his identity has come back in horror. Now he sees the utter folly of his claim to be the master and interpreter of nature: "I perceive I have not really understood any thing—not a single object—and that no man ever can." He is and always has been in the hands of mysterious great forces that save him as they please and drop him as they please.

The poem bears every mark of having been written by a man in deep grief, as indeed it was. Strangely, the whole scene is in distress and mourns with the poet even while it denies him. The wound of separation pains both alike. Its cause is mysterious, but we vaguely sense some unspecified hurt behind the vastation they lament. All we know is that the blow has been struck and he finds himself here, crushed and abandoned. The poem denies the claims of "Song of Myself" much more radically than did "The Sleepers." Whitman confronts annihilation once more, not in the guise of dreams but in waking earnest, just as if his visions of life had never been. "(See! from my dead lips the ooze exuding at last!)" The transcendental cycle is over. He hopes, it is true, that "the flow will return" and that he "will yet sing, someday," but this must be read as prayer, not conviction. Though he may yet in a measure recover his spirits and his singing strength, the sweeping affirmative power from which his first-phase poems had proceeded will never return in that form again.

Rather he finds a way out on the other side of his despair itself. We can watch this happen in one of the most extraordinary poems he ever wrote, "Scented Herbage of My Breast." This, like "As I Ebb'd," is another farewell to his vocation as the poet of Life—

indeed, to life itself. The poet, anticipating the death he now welcomes, thinks of his "leaves," no longer as the grass growing even on graves to show "there is really no death," but as delicate "tomb-leaves" that will survive for a while the killing winter, as he cannot, to bloom perennially from his grave and tell "a few" of the suffering from which they sprang. The poem is itself a "breast leaf" of the kind it describes, a solitary cry of grief like the song of the bird in "Out of the Cradle." It soon drops its elegiac tone and speaks out directly.

> O aching and throbbing! O these hungering desires!
> Surely one day they will be pacified—all will be accomplished
> O I know not what you mean—you are not happiness—you
>   are often too bitter!

The interpolated assurance here, an echo of his old faith, is now purely a desperate expression of need. The true ground of his pain is the recognition that *nothing* will pacify his desires, that love is necessarily something unaccomplished. Why this must be so becomes clear when we remember what Whitman meant by love. He has been shown at last what real love is only to find that it is something that cannot and must not hope for fulfillment. Since love is also the only real thing in life, the heart of this poem is a genuinely tragic recognition: to live is to love and to love is to lose. Love is the beginning of life and also its end. Whitman has moved in this poem beyond the personal torment of such a Calamus poem as "Hours Continuing Long" to a universal insight.

Not that "Scented Herbage" is any the less passionate for that; it is the most passionate love poem he ever wrote. His recognition lifts him to a kind of exaltation. Death becomes beautiful to him, not because it promises him the fulfillment life denies him, but simply because his love is so strong that it must go somewhere and this is the only way open to it. Since to love is to lose, "the high Soul of lovers welcomes death most." Life reserves for the lover its final secret, that the "real reality" is love and death. The poem rises to meet the new knowledge that the needs of the heart are not met by life, that man is born for defeat. The only course open to him, then, is to consent to what must be, cast off his demand for life and fear of death and go to meet his fate halfway. "Death or life I am then indifferent—my Soul declines to prefer." Its exaltation is the exaltation of passing beyond hope and illusion to a knowledge of what life and death finally are. "The readiness is all."

> He is King of Harm
> Who hath suffered Him.

I have suggested that at the peak of his transcendental vision Whitman knew immortality by direct insight, with no need for the aid of myth or doctrine. Something like that is true at this second peak also. The knowledge to which this poem rises of love and death as the real reality is without intermediary or metaphor.

> Emblematic and capricious blades, I leave you—now you
>   serve me not,
> Away! I will say what I have to say, by itself. . . .

If there is such a thing as tragic Reason, then this is its poem. Death is welcomed, not because of any promise or myth, nor through mere despair of life, but simply in and for itself, because it is real.

It would be pleasant to ring down the curtain on this high note, as on one of the soaring fifth-act arias which this poem much resembles, but with thirty years of Whitman's work and at least one of his greatest poems still to come that would hardly be accurate. This kind of vision, too, like all vision, has its laws and limits. One difference between art and life is that the tragic hero can remain frozen on his peak of exaltation while the actual man must come down from such heights and go on living. Whitman, I would guess, found it much harder to hold to his tragic vision in its purity than he had found it to maintain his transcendental one. It seems likely that only an extraordinary stress of feeling brought him to the point of such vision at all; as that stress diminished he never quite reached it again, though if my thesis is correct its impact decisively controls all his later work.

A "dialectical" pattern of emotional development much like that which reached its definitive artistic expression in "When Lilacs Last," I am arguing, was a central pattern in his own experience, *lived through* by him well before he ever looked into Hegel. From the simultaneous knowledge of the ever-present immortality and of the event of death, the transcendental assurance and its demonic shadow, each dominant in turn according to the strength or weakness of his vision of safety, he moved, under the impact of his awakening to love and death, to a new knowledge both sadder and surer. If there was loss in the collapse of his total triumph over death, there was gain in the certainty that no further shock of awakening could come to him; now he *knew.* The ground of the recovery which, as Asselineau argues, the very publication of the 1860 edition attests was thus laid by the same discovery that destroyed the overconfidence out of which his poems had begun. The knowledge it brought him, the stoic privilege it gave him of being one of those that know the truth, became the rock on which his mature equilibrium thereafter was founded. His wound-dressing years tested and confirmed it but did not create it.

A similar process of confirmation can be traced in the poems. Since it brought him at last to assurances of immortality that superficially resemble his first-phase proclamations and which in his final philosophic phase, when he wished to insist on the synthetic unity of his whole work, he was glad to merge with them, it is important to insist that they do not have the same basis. Whitman did not just "recover his serenity," if by that we mean that all became as it had been. The greatest disservice the later Whitman did himself was to lead us to overlook and belittle the significance of his deepest crisis. After he "had been to touch the great death," he could no longer reach, and no longer needed, the power to affirm that death did not exist. He never again looked for final satisfaction to life, nor did he again fall under the old terror of annihilation.

What happened instead was that he began instincitvely to build on his new insight, as he had his old, with imaginative materials, to bolster and confirm it, if also somewhat to ease it, with "carols of death" more suitable to the needs of the Understanding. Since metaphors for the Understanding are the lifeblood of poetry it appears foolish to complain of this process and indeed I do not. Many of its results, such as "Darest Thou Now, O Soul" or "Whispers of Heavenly Death" or "Reconciliation," not to mention "When Lilacs Last," are particularly beautiful, so that one would be grateful for Whitman's Calamus crisis if it had led to nothing else. It is a measure of his achievement in "Scented Herbage" to suggest that such poems are in any sense deficient by comparison. On a level just below them is a poem like "Passage to India," one of the best of Whitman's second-best poems, where the metaphor has begun to shrink and harden into a relatively conventional doctrine of the soul's immortal safety on "the seas of God" beyond the grave. We can catch this mythologizing process at its inception and perhaps at its best in "Out of the Cradle."

III

In "Out of the Cradle" Whitman has contrived to tell his whole story and even to go beyond it. The long one-sentence "pre-verse" is intended to establish the basic fiction of the poem. The poet will tell us of something long past, he suggests, which now for some reason comes over his memory. By this distancing device he contrives to win some artistic and personal control over his material. In most versions the distinction of the poet that is and the boy that was is made sharp and distinct:

I, chanter of pains and joys, uniter of here and hereafter . . .
A reminiscence sing.

Such a bardic line implies firm poetic control, emotion recollected in tranquillity. But neither this line nor the following one is in the 1859 version, where the poet therefore seems much more under the spell of the memories that have seized him:

A man—yet by these tears a little boy again,
Throwing myself on the sand, I,
Confronting the waves, sing.

What has actually seized him, of course, is the meaning *now* to him of these images, so much so that in the first version he has a hard time keeping the presentness of his feelings from bursting through and destroying his narrative fiction.

Nevertheless, the reminiscent mode of the poem greatly enlarges its range by permitting him to bring his whole life to bear on it. As a poem of loss and awakening it goes back even to his very earliest loss and awakening, the "primal" separation of the child from the mother. Though this theme is stressed at once by the poet, especially in the original version, one must avoid reductiveness here. This layer of the poem underlies the whole and already predicts its shape, but it is not the completed structure. From it comes, however, a powerful metaphor for the awakening that is the main subject.

The boy, leaving his bed, finds himself wandering in a strange dark world like something out of Blake, a haunted borderland between shore and sea, here and hereafter, conscious and unconscious. In its troubled restlessness it resembles the moonlit swamp that is glimpsed for a moment in "Song of Myself," or some of the dream-scenes in "The Sleepers." We sense here, especially in the 1859 version, which is more dark and troubled throughout than the final one, the same dumb, unassuageable grief as in "As I Ebb'd." It also is a wounded world, impotently twining and twisting with the pain of some obscure fatality. Here there is even less visible occasion for such agony, since the chief actor is not a broken poet but a curious child. The poem is heavy with the man's foreknowledge of what the child, now born, must go through. Like the star in "When Lilacs Last," however, the scene also has something to tell, some "drowned secret" which it is struggling to utter. It does not merely mourn a loss, like the sea-scape in "As I Ebb'd," but also hints of something to be found.

What has drawn the boy from his infantile security into this parturient midnight is a bird. In a flashback the poet tells of the brief May idyll of Two Together, the sudden loss of the she-bird, and the wonderful song of woe that followed, drawing the boy back night after night to listen until the night came when he awakened to its meaning. Then it seemed to him that the bird was a messenger, an interpreter, singing on behalf of the new world he had entered to tell him its secret. This secret is really two secrets, that the meaning of life is love and that he is to be its poet. The song releases the love and the songs of love in his own heart, which he now realizes has long been ready and waiting for this moment; he awakes and ecstatically dedicates himself to this service.

Yet, bewilderingly, this discovery of what life means and what he is for at once plunges him into new trouble and doubt; he finds himself once more groping for something unknown, and is not released until the voice of the sea whispers him a very different secret, the word death. This *double* awakening provides criticism with its chief problem in this poem. It is true that the boy's spiritual development is dramatically consistent and requires no explanation from outside the poem, but it is complex and rapid, an extreme example of dramatic foreshortening. Since it is also intensely personal, the biographical framework I have sketched helps to make its meaning clear.

To put the matter summarily, in the boy's awakening Whitman has fused all his own awakenings together, with the result that his poem moves in one night over a distance which he had taken forty years of life to cover. The emotional foreground, of course, is occupied by the tragic awakening of 1859, the discovery of love not merely as a passion for one particular being rather than an appetite for everything in general, but also as inherently unsatisfied. Love and grief are one. The bird's story is Whitman's story, distanced and disguised, but it is also man's. The outsetting bard of love will be the bard of unsatisfied love because there is no other kind.

But here we encounter a difficulty, for in many of the other poems of 1859 Whitman had suggested that his awakening to love had stopped his poems and ended his poetic career. Of course he could hardly have overlooked the fact that his crisis did arouse him to new poems and to some of his best. Certainly he was proud of this poem, immediately printed it and followed it with one of his self-written reviews announcing that he would not be mute any more. Perhaps we may read a special meaning into his selection of this poem as the first public evidence of his return to song. In this "reminiscence" of the birth of his poetic vocation he is actually celebrating its recovery. The process of relieving his pain in song has now proceeded so far, past "death's outlet" songs like "Hours Continuing Long" and "As I Ebb'd," past a poem of first recognition like "Scented Herbage," that he can now begin to see that the deathblow to his old "arrogant poems" is proving to be a lifeblow to new and better if more sorrowful ones, and so for the first time, in the guise of a reminiscence, he can make not just his grief but its transmutation into the relief of song the subject of his singing.

In the measure that he recovers his poetic future he also recovers his past. His sense of returning powers naturally picks up and blends with his memories of that other awakening, whenever and

whatever it was, that led to the poems of 1855. In the boy's joy
he draws on and echoes his first awakening, the ecstatic union of
self and soul celebrated in "Song of Myself," when he *had* felt a
thousand songs starting to life within him in response to the
"song of Two Together." Overlaid on that is his second dark
awakening to the truth of "two together no more" which had at
first appeared to end his singing. If we thus provisionally dis-
entangle the strands that Whitman has woven together we can
understand better why the song of the bird must plunge the boy
almost simultaneously into ecstasy and despair.

The steps of this process are obscured for us in the final version
by Whitman's deletion of a crucial stanza that explains why the
boy needs a word from the sea when he already has so much from
the bird. After the lines

> O give me some clue!
> O if I am to have so much, let me have more!

the original version continued as follows:

> O a word! O what is my destination?
> O I fear it is henceforth chaos!
> O how joys, dreads, convolutions, human shapes, and all
>   shapes, spring as from graves around me!
> O phantoms! You cover all the land and all the sea!
> O I cannot see in the dimness whether you smile or frown
>   upon me!
> O vapor, a look, a word! O well-beloved!
> O you dear women's and men's phantoms!

This stanza or something similar appears in all editions of "Out
of the Cradle" until the last version of 1881, when Whitman was

twenty years away from his poem. Perhaps he dropped it then because he felt it spoke too plainly from the emotions of 1859 and was not in keeping with what his poem had become. That it was not necessary to the success of the poem is proved by the success the poem has had without it, yet its omission greatly changes the total effect. The quality of the boy's need is lightened to a more usual adolescent distress and the sea's answer becomes the kind of grave reassurance characteristic of the later Whitman. In the original version the boy is not just distressed, he is desperate with the desperation of the man of 1859. The first act of his awakened poet's vision has been to abort and produce a frightening chaos. Instead of the triumphant vision of Life which Whitman himself had known, when the whole world smiled on its conquering lover, nothing rises now before the outsetting bard but a dim phantasmagoria of death-shapes. It is almost impossible not to read this passage as coming from the poet himself rather than from the boy—indeed, Whitman was right to cut it, it *is* out of keeping—for these "dear women's and men's phantoms" are surely dear because they are those of the men and women and the whole world that had *already* started to life for him in his poems, their life the eddying of his living soul, but are now strengthless ghosts, like the power of vision from which their life had come. This is the "terrible doubt of appearances" that had plagued him from the beginning, now revived and confirmed by his new crisis. Whitman here openly transfers to the boy the man's despair.

With this background it should not be hard to see that the answer the sea gives to the despair characteristic of 1859 is the answer characteristic of 1859. Its essential quality is the same tragic acceptance as in "Scented Herbage," a knowledge of death not as consolation or promise, still less as mere appearance, but as reality, the "real reality" that completes the reality of love in the only way in which it can be completed. In the language of Thoreau, the sea is a "realometer" that says, "this is, and no mistake." The lift her answer brings is like that of "Scented Herbage," the lift of naming the whole truth and so passing beyond illusion to a consent to fate. A sign that this is so is the sea's taciturnity. The thrush's beautiful song of death in 1865, weaving a veil of life-illusion over the same hard truth and so easing it for us, is not present here; simply the word, the thing itself. In this stark directness, again, the kinship is to "Scented Herbage" rather than to "When Lilacs Last." ·

Yet certainly the fact that this word also, like the bird's song of love and the boy's despair, is ascribed to a dramatic character makes a profound difference. The sea as dramatic character in this poem has two phases. In the earlier part, before the boy turns to her for his answer, she is a background voice blending with the drama of bird and boy but essentially not a part of it. She has an ancient sorrow of her own which leaves her no grief to spare for this small incident on her shores. She does not share the egocentric fallacy of boy and bird, in which even moon, wind, and shadows join in futile sympathy. In this part of the poem she is the same sea as in "As I Ebb'd," the "fierce old mother" who "endlessly cries for her castaways"—all her castaways, not just these —the deep ocean of life and death that rolls through all things.

Of course, behind every detail of the poem, including this one, we feel the poet's shaping power, creating a symbolical language for the life of his own mind. In this kind of subjective drama the author is all the characters; bird, boy, and sea are one and join in a grief that is at bottom the same because it is his own. But Whitman has now seen through the Emersonian illusion that the power of the poet prophesies a victory for the man. Where "Song of Myself" had dramatized the omnipotence of bardic vision, "Out of the Cradle" dramatizes the discovery that the power of the bard is only to sing his own limits. Like the bird in Marianne Moore's poem, his singing is mighty because he is caged. As a dramatic character, then, the sea is the Not-Me, Fate, Karma, that-which-cannot-be-changed. As such she dominates the scene, which is all, as Kenneth Burke would say, under her aegis, but she does not share in its temporal passions.

At the end, however, she condescends to reveal herself and changes from the ground of the question to the answer. The change is not so much in the sea as in the boy. As before, he hears when he is ready to listen; the sea has been speaking all the time. Even the bird, in the early version, heard her and responded with continued song. Before he can hear her the boy must finish his egocentric cycle and pass from his hybristic promise to sing "clearer, louder, and more sorrowful" songs than the bird's to his despairing recognition that there is no good in him. The sign that he is ready is the question itself. Then the sea approaches and whispers as privately for him, revealing the secret which will release him from passion to perception. What she shows him is, I have suggested, no consoling revelation but simply reality. Yet the fact that this answer is now felt to come from the sea, from the heart of the Not-Me that has defeated Whitman's arrogant demands for another Me, suggests that the division between him and his world is not final after all, that the separation both have suffered can still be healed. The elemental forces of "As I Ebb'd" have fused with the perception of reality in "Scented Herbage" to form a new Thou, in Buber's language—no longer the tousled mistress Whitman had ordered around in "Song of Myself," certainly, but a goddess who will speak to him when he is ready to accept her on her own terms. Then he can hear in the voice of the sea the voice of a mother, a figure as we know "always near and always divine" to him. The real reality of "Scented Herbage" has acquired a local habitation and a name, has gathered around itself life and numenosity, and Whitman is well on his way by this dark path to replace the Comrade who had deserted him on the open road.

Paul Fussell, Jr.

WHITMAN'S CURIOUS WARBLE:

REMINISCENCE AND RECONCILIATION

> Even as a boy, I had the fancy, the wish, to write a piece, perhaps a
> poem, about the sea-shore—that suggesting, dividing line, contact, junc-
> tion, the solid marrying the liquid—that curious, lurking something,
> (as doubtless every objective form finally becomes to the subjective
> spirit,) which means far more than its mere first sight, grand as that is
> —blending the real and ideal, and each made portion of the other.
>   "How I Still Get Around at Sixty and Take Notes" (1881)

The current Whitman revival, which has been both registered
and stimulated by the recent writings of Randall Jarrell, Leslie
Fiedler, and Richard Chase, seems to have drawn much sus-
tenance from a sharpened recognition of the conventional element of artifice in all poems and of the fictive element in all
poetical careers. Because recent biographical findings, notably
Gay Wilson Allen's, have reminded us that the gulf between the
actual and the poetical biography is as wide in Whitman as in most
writers of poems, we are beginning to learn how to redeem Whitman from life, from politics, and from folk philosophy. Pope
tells us in his poems that his own satiric motives are noble and
disinterested, and that his father is saintly; Whitman tells us that
he witnessed interesting things during a trip to Nevada, and that

his mother is a perfect specimen. Both are exercising themselves in the art of telling lies successfully. When Whitman asserts in "Out of the Cradle Endlessly Rocking" that it was in the month of May that the male mockingbird enjoyed his female, and that he bemoaned the loss of her until the month of September, or when he tells us that the boy in his poem experienced his seashore epiphany just before dawn, we shall find out what is going on in the poem more successfully by inquiring into the way poems in general work and by consulting the conventions of certain kinds of poems than by inquiring into matters of bird migrations or into the details of Whitman's early life near the Long Island beaches.

Although we may not wish to proceed in this direction so precipitately as Northrop Frye, who declares that "poetry can only be made out of other poems," I think that few any longer will feel disillusioned to be reminded that if Whitman is a poet, he is then preeminently not a person to whom certain experiences happen but rather a person who has learned the tactics of constructing certain recognizable verbal artifacts; and that his artifacts will be permanent to the degree that they resemble not the unlicked episodes of actual experience but the significant shapes of a world of universal forms. If we have learned anything as critics in the past fifty years, what we have learned is to welcome artificial golden birds that warble mechanically in expensive golden trees; we are learning likewise not merely to accept but actually to rejoice in butterflies manufactured of cardboard. Whitman's "pose" is less his personal property than an inevitable property of the world of poems.

In approaching "Out of the Cradle Endlessly Rocking," we may thus dismiss at the outset questions of Whitman's assumed "lost lover," thought by some to lie behind the making of the poem; we may relieve ourselves of the task of speculating whether the voice of the bird in the poem represents the voice of the opera-singer Marietta Alboni; we may even disregard questions of what actually happened to Whitman to impel him to "record" his presumed experience in this poem. I do not want to deny that Whitman had an experience; I merely want to assert that the only valuable experience the poem offers us is a wholly artistic one.

Turning, then, from biographical to artistic questions, we may begin by asking what kind of a poem we have here: what is its genre? Most obviously, it is related to the standard Romantic lyric of reminiscence whose theme is the origin in boyhood of the lyric impulse and its precarious maintenance into a cooler world of manhood. Wordsworth's "Ode: Intimations of Immortality" provides, perhaps, the clearest analogue. Robert D. Faner suggests that the poem is really a sort of miniature Italian opera without music, both in structure (that is, alternating recitative and aria, which culminate in a mode of ensemble) and in theme (that is, the theme, sacred to early-nineteenth-century Italian opera, of consummated love followed by separation and death). Again, Northrop Frye, by suggesting that the poem of "emblematic vision," as he calls it, is a complex development of the genre of the riddle, gives us a means for a fresh apprehension of the importance of Whitman's lines 158–159:

> O give me the clew! (it lurks in the night here somewhere,)
> O if I am to have so much, let me have more!

Although these are useful approaches, we can perhaps go further by conceiving of the poem as a very American exercise, both in theme and in occasion and method. In theme it resembles the representative American work in which a boy like Huck Finn or Ishmael or Nick Adams or Ike McCaslin, positioned in the midst of physical nature, discovers the idea of death and then enacts some strategic ritual by which his discovery is brought into coherence with his journey toward maturity. In this sense the poem resembles a memorializing of an initiation ritual; and it is the artistic imitation of this ritual that the American writer seems hardly able to avoid at some point in his career: James's Isabel Archer as well as Fitzgerald's Nick Carraway come immediately to mind.

In its occasion and method as well the poem appears to belong to an American genre. Because we seem to need a name for this kind of poem, I suggest the term *The American Shore Ode*. The characteristics of this kind of poem are these: it is a lyric of some length and philosophic density spoken (usually at a specific place) on an American beach; its theme tends to encompass the relationship of the wholeness and flux of the sea to the discreteness and fixity of land objects. This kind of poem does more than simply engage in transcendental meditations about the sea: the important thing is the dissimilarity between shore and sea, sand and water, separateness and cohesiveness, analysis and synthesis —a dissimilarity which explains and justifies their paradoxical marriage. The proximity of briers to ocean in Eliot's "The Dry Salvages" ("the salt is on the briar rose") and Whitman's "Out of the Cradle" ("Out from the patches of briers . . . I . . . A reminiscense sing") is a detail reminding us that we might consider Eliot's poem as belonging to this genre. And so might we consider such poems as Lanier's "The Marshes of Glynn"; Longfellow's "Seaweed" and "The Tide Rises, the Tide Falls"; Emerson's "Seashore"; Trumbull Stickney's "At Sainte-Marguerite"; Hilda Doolittle's "Sea Gods," Jeffers's "Night," Crane's "Voyages," Howard Baker's "Ode to the Sea," Marianne Moore's "A Grave," and Stevens's "The Idea of Order at Key West." Although Pound's Canto II does not, clearly, occur on Long Island, its sharp sense of the relationship of sea to shore may be thought to betray, if not its genre, at least its essential nationality. Even Frost's unpretentious "Neither Out Far nor in Deep," William Meredith's "The Open Sea," and Josephine Miles's eight-line poem "Career" ("Who run the sea wall in diapers/ Look to their job") seem close to this genre. And I would suggest that the reasons why the Shore Ode seems an American kind of poem are less topographical than philosophic. The shore-surf relationship provides the American imagination with a naturalistic "uniform hieroglyphic" of a Romantic reconciliation of dualisms: the relationship can serve as an emblem of the reconciliation of separate states with the idea of a federal union; it can provide an image of the reconciliation of the aristocratic inner world of solipsistic singularity with the democratic outer world of perceptual uniformity, or, in Whitman's terms, a reconciling of the "simple separate person" with the "En-Masse"; and finally (and this is the most important use of the image for a New World, non-Christian sensibility like Whitman's), it can serve as a means of reconciling, without recourse to sacred history, love with loss, life with death, time with eternity. The fundamental shore-sea image of this kind of basic American poem makes significant appearances even in novels: at the beginning of *Moby-Dick* Ishmael points out to us the thousands of "mortal men" (the adjective is important) who peer seaward from the edges of Manhattan on "a dreamy Sabbath afternoon"; "nothing will content them," we are told, "but the extremest limit of the land." And we remember Hemingway's Jake Barnes, who, after the orgy of mortality and losses at Pamplona, betakes himself in solitude to the beach at San Sebastian. Whether we encounter it in poem or novel, the shore-sea image appears to lie very near the heart of the American contemplative and speculative experience. I do not intend to imply that Whitman, a helpless victim of a sort of determinism of thematic and formal archetypes, is obliged to write this kind of poem; but I am trying to imply that, given his nationality and his philosophic predispositions, Whitman could have put together "Out of the Cradle Endlessly Rocking" almost as satisfactorily if, instead of wending as a boy the shores he knew, he had frequented a library and quietly hummed Emma Hart Willard's "Rocked in the Cradle of the Deep" while adapting the dualistic formulations of Hegel, Coleridge, and Wordsworth to the new anatomies of the American circumstance.

Once we begin to perceive what kind of a poem is before us, we are ready to attend to its details and structure. Coming upon the metric of the first line, we observe its absolute symmetry and regularity: one way of expressing it would be to say that a dactyl and a trochee are separated by a caesura from a dactyl and a trochee. Regardless of the technical terms we use, we will see that the metrical balance of the two metrically equal halves of the line is as artfully contrived as if the line had been written for a seventeenth-century French tragedy. If the metrical pattern at the beginning of the first line sounds familiar to us, it does so perhaps because the first four syllables of the line create a cadence (resembling the classical choriambus) which is one of the most frequent in Whitman's poems, and to which he is so devoted that it almost becomes the metrical hallmark of the standard Whitman title, even in his prose: it is the pattern we hear behind "Song of Myself" and *Specimen Days;* and behind the first four syllables of "Song of the Open Road," "Passage to India," "Notes of a Half-Paralytic," "Children of Adam," "Song of the Broad-Axe," "Prayer of Columbus," and "Whispers of Heavenly Death." The sophisticated impulse toward symmetrical structure that impelled Whitman to revise the abrupt and conversational "Out of the rocked cradle" of the first version is just as apparent in his management of the larger details of the whole structure. As Fredson Bowers concludes after a precise textual study of many of the MSS of the third edition (1860) of *Leaves of Grass,* "These poems were built, for all their air of carefree extemporaneousness."

Lines 1 to 22 constitute a richly orchestrated prologue, and, in addition, contain in one important cluster of images (lines 18–22) a kind of version in miniature of the poem as a whole. The strange prepositional suspensions and the extravagant periodic structure of the one initial sentence charge the opening with an illusion of excitement and breathlessness; and the very reiterated curiousness of the prepositional idiom reinforces the portentousness of the moonlit, dreamlike setting. What the speaker begins by saying is that he sings a reminiscence not "of" or "about" a number of particulars for which he once found the "key" to fuse into a whole significant experience; he sings instead a reminiscence *"out of"* these particulars. The "out of" suggests an image of conscious and purposive extraction, of a muscular squeezing of meaning from discrete phenomena, the way one would squeeze juice from a handful of grapes. Here the purposiveness and vigor of the activity of memory clearly distinguish the occasion from one of daydreaming or accidental imagining. The intellectual occasion here is not one of a static loafing and inviting the soul: it is a conscious backward journeying, a quest, like that in Frost's "Directive," solemnly undertaken by means of the rituals appropriate to it.

Taking the first twenty-two lines as a unit, we may begin by paraphrasing thus: "I, made by this experience into a coherent man-boy; now through this remembered experience able to contrive poems reconciling man's present state with his post-mortal future; I, now become a poet capable through this experience of reconciling the hopeless with the hopeful; I record here a reminiscence of a meaningful moment from my past, a reminiscence compounded of a number of disparate phenomena which cohere in my memory to suggest the way they can be fixed in poetic form. I make my poem by extracting significance from the following recalled particulars: the endlessly moving sea and breaking waves; the instinctual sound-box ('musical shuttle') of the male mockingbird; and the September midnight when I finally began to attain this revelation; I draw significance from 'over' the sands where the boy 'I' wandered barefoot in darkness; I extract significance both 'down from' the distant, inaccessible (because vaguely holy) luminous ring ('halo') around the moon, and 'out from' the nearby, accessible beach plants and their shadows. Reconciling and fusing my present moment of composition with my past moment of epiphany, I make my poem from my past experience and my present memories of the mockingbird's song of love and loss, of life and death; and from my past experience and my present memories of what that song taught me about poetic themes and techniques. Even more important, I make central use in my poem of my memory of 'the word' *death,* 'stronger and more delicious than any' other word or symbol. So packed with meaning are the materials I recall that their mere cataloguing starts me revisiting the scene already: they are carrying me back there hurriedly before I am fully prepared." And now, at line 18, we come upon a miniature, compressed version of the primary argument of the whole poem:

> A man, yet by these tears a little boy again,
> Throwing myself on the sand, confronting the waves,
> I, chanter of pains and joys, uniter of here and hereafter,
> Taking all hints to use them [the details which the reminis-
>   cence is being extracted "out of"], but swiftly leaping
>   beyond them,
> A reminiscence sing.

The action of the poem, which is a quest through purposive reminiscence arriving, finally, at the reconciliation of opposites, appears to be almost totally figured forth in these five lines, where the sand becomes an emblem of the "here" (or time) and the sea of the "hereafter" (or eternity). "Pains," likewise, are associated with the un-unified and thus initially meaningless particulars of the beach (that is, the *"sterile* sands," the *"patches* of briers and blackberries," and "the mystic play of *shadows,"* shadows which, as the speaker's mode of simile tells us, are really quite fixed and dead but which twine and twist *as if* they were alive). The beach is seen as the world of mutually isolated phenomena, lifeless and insignificant in their lonely discreteness; it bears a kinship with the ashen and gritty world of Carlyle's "Everlasting No," of Arnold's "Dover Beach," and even of Eliot's

"Waste Land." But the waves, confronted once by the boy and now once again in memory by the man-boy, are associated paradoxically both with infinite nonidentity and, at the same time, with infinite joys and the hereafter. Operating through the juxtapositioning of these dualistic images, lines 18–22 thus pose the problem of the poem: implicitly they ask the question, How are sand and waves, analysis and synthesis, time and eternity, pains and joys, here and hereafter to be fused? And line 18 ("A man, yet by these tears a little boy again") foreshadows the sublimely successful self-union (to use Emerson's term for it) between boyhood and maturity which the poem enacts in the very last section (lines 174–183).

It is this anticipation of the end of the poem in its beginning, this prefiguring of the final triumph in the tight image-cluster (lines 18–20) of the boy prone on the sands confronting the waves, that Whitman seems to be calling attention to in his coyly anonymous remarks on the poem, remarks published on the editorial page of the *Saturday Press* for December 27, 1859, where the poem made its first appearance illogically titled "A Child's Reminiscence":

WALT WHITMAN'S POEM

Our readers may, if they choose, consider as our Christmas or New Year's present to them, the curious warble, by Walt Whitman, of "A Child's Reminiscence," on our First Page. Like the "Leaves of Grass," the purport of this wild and plaintive song, well-enveloped and eluding definition, is positive and unquestionable, like the effect of music.

The piece will bear reading many times—perhaps, indeed, only comes forth, as from recesses, by many repetitions.

Although Whitman's phrase "well-enveloped" implies that the "purport" of the poem is so dense as to "elude" immediate "definition," it suggests also that the central portion of the poem (lines 23-173) is enveloped by a structural envelope in which the experience is first anticipated and then recapitulated. Again, it is apparent that the poem is built out of two kinds of discourse, and we find that an envelope of "recitative" (that is, relatively discursive utterance, or man-song) surrounds a unified core of central "aria" (that is, florid, apostrophic, lyric utterance, or birdsong). The effect of the over-all envelope structure is to suggest a now permanent containment of the one kind of rhetoric within the other; or, to put it another way, to suggest a reconciliation of two opposed modes of utterance, the unconscious and the conscious, the instinctual mode of "the musical shuttle" and the artful, painfully learned mode of the human voice engaged in rhetorical stratagems. We might even entertain the simplification that the reconciliation effected by the "well-enveloped" structure is one between lyric and epic modes. That is, the rhetorical characteristics which the structure attempts to fuse are the traditional orderliness of narration, or epic, with the traditional impulsiveness of apostrophe, or lyric. If the poem does succeed in effecting a marriage between these two modes, we may say that it consummates for one intense and brilliant moment (lines 175-178) a rare union between the Aristotelian and the Longinian senses of literature.

After the twenty-two-line prologue and anticipation, the speaker provides narrative background in nine lines presented in suspended participial syntax. The mode of syntax here operates as if the action were not completed, as indeed, in one sense, it will not be until near the end of the poem (line 144), when we burst forth from a complex of largely incomplete participial suspensions into a fully coherent universe of discourse in full predication. In these nine lines of narrative background (lines 23-31) the speaker places the beginning of the recollected action in May among images of fecundity: the lilac scent is in the air, the conventional Whitmanian grass is growing, and, couched among the briers on the shore, two mockingbirds from the amply more fertile South wait for the hatching of their eggs.

The cycle of the birds' love is almost complete, and in the next section, a nine-line "aria," the male bird delivers from his musical shuttle an impulsive apostrophic lyric, an instinctual address of ecstasy to the sun. Considered wholly by itself, the he-bird's first aria appears simple enough, but seen in context, it accumulates irony. The burden of the song is a complacent and pitifully optimistic celebration of the permanence of joy. The solitary singer assures himself that "While we two keep together," experience will be a matter of "Singing all time, minding no time." But ironically, "time" is one of the "pains" to be "minded," as the abrupt transition to the recitative passage which follows (lines 41-51) makes clear. This eleven-line narrative passage, announcing the unanticipated disappearance of the female bird and the gradually increasing anxiety both of the male bird and of the observing barefoot boy, is couched in an ambiguous syntax which repays close inspection. For in line 49 we find the ambiguous participle "flitting," which modifies at once both "I" and "the remaining one, the he-bird": already in the poem boy and bird are drawing together, as they must if the predicament of the one is to be readily "translated" (cf. line 31) into terms apprehensible by the other.

Although the boy does not yet consciously recognize the bird as his "dusky demon and brother" (line 175), he does now "flit" birdlike "from brier to brier by day," "cautiously peering" (cf. line 31) out of hiding the way the bird peers in search of his mate.

Just as the bird's joyous first aria consisted in an apostrophe to the sun, so his second aria (lines 52–54) is an apostrophe to the south wind, which he exhorts to "blow my mate to me." Despite a certain distress in its tone, the male bird's second aria is still full of hope, for he seems to assume that he knows where his mate has gone—she has, he imagines, slipped momentarily home to Alabama. But the reader is already fully aware of the dramatic irony, for he has been carefully told by the speaker back in line 45 that the she-bird did not return, "Nor ever appear'd again." It was on a morning in spring that the female disappeared; all summer long the male reiterates his naively hopeful lyric, which changes finally, near the end of summer, into the important central aria (lines 71–129).

The speaker prepares for this major instinctual utterance by setting the scene precisely in lines 55–70. Here we are placed in a posture for listening by exact descriptive images: the stars are glistening; the he-bird rests "All night long on the prong of a moss-scallop'd stake,/ Down almost amid the slapping waves." It will be noticed that the mockingbird, conspicuously a creature of the land rather than the sea, is positioned closer to the sea as his final recognition of the actuality of his loss becomes more and more apparent to him. The "slapping waves" seem to transmit to the bird something very close to what, in lines 165–173, they transmit to the boy, who also, in his turn, must move closer to the sea for its intelligence to reach him. But although the bird is almost as close to the sea as the boy will be subsequently, the "key," the "clew" from the "liquid rims," does not reveal itself to the bird. In lines 61–70 the speaker tries to explain why he, of all people, is able to understand and "translate" the import of the bird's central elegy. "He pour'd forth the meanings which I of all men know": notice that the speaker does not know the meanings because he has also lost a lover (he is, we recall, "a little boy"); he knows the meanings for two other reasons. First, the bird's song of loss "tallies" naturally with the boy's sense of melancholy and with his search for his own coherence and identity; and second, the curious and sympathetic boy took pains to hear the song of the bird repeated all summer long; the song has worked on the boy through repetition—he has listened to it "more than once" (line 63) and "long and long" (line 68).

The bird's central aria exhibits its own self-contained rhetorical action. It begins in erotic reminiscence, proceeds to the extraction of a desperate hope from any quarter, and moves finally in total despair to a recognition of perpetual loss. The aria stands thus as a sort of significantly incomplete image of "Out of the Cradle" as a whole: not being human, the bird lacks the capacity for symbol-making; he ends in a puzzled awareness of both loss and the sea, but he is unable to combine idea with image to break through, as the speaker finally does, into an ecstatic awareness of total coherence and acceptance.

This aria begins, like the two brief anticipatory arias preceding, in apostrophe; and now it is the sea, rather than the sun or the wind, which is addressed. In lines 71–80 the bird dwells on the action of the surf in rhythmically soothing both itself and its opposite, the sand. The bird's design here is apparently to use the erotic surf-sand image as a pretext for indulging a joyful reminiscence of his own past erotic joys. This erotic meditation provides the bird with the motive for seeking his love again, and, in lines 79–80, he begs the night to reassure him that his love is indeed returning, is "that little black thing I see there in the white" of the breakers. After an excited and hopeful address (lines 81–85) to his absent mate, in which the bird assures his mate that he is still there, waiting, he turns to apostrophize the moon. The moon is somehow sympathetic with the bird's loss: it is seen as "heavy with unsatisfied love," as "low-hanging," "lagging," and, later, as "drooping." But despite its sympathy with the bird's predicament, the moon is silent and self-contained: it offers no "key" or "clew" to the bird. Here the image of the lost female as a dark spot against brightness is repeated: "What," the bird inquires of the moon, "is that dusky spot in your brown yellow?" Receiving no "clew" from the moon, the bird turns with an increasing anxiety to apostrophize both the land behind him and the stars overhead. They too, like the sun, wind, sea, and moon, are wordless and self-composed. They have no answers for a bird's inquiries. Moving now to consider the possibility that the fault is his rather than nature's, and that perhaps he is not singing loudly or clearly enough, the bird exhorts his own throat to "sound clearer," to "pierce the woods, the earth." And he next goes so far as to apostrophize his own songs—he exhorts them to trill ("shake out") correctly, as if he has now come to doubt even his own technical competence.

Lines 105–110 exhibit the bird desperately torn between a desire to listen for a possible response from his love and a desire not to stop singing lest his love miss him. He resolves this dilemma in lines 111–114 by deciding to maintain a "just sustain'd note," "a gentle call," so soft that he will be able to hear above it an answering song. But now that he has lowered his voice, he recognizes in lines 115–118 another difficulty: the trouble now is that his "just sustain'd note" will so closely resemble the whistling of the wind and the fluttering of the spray that its uniqueness in nature will be unrecognizable.

At line 119, the exhausted and now spiritless bird arrives at his final perception. He has begun by indulging, perhaps unwisely, erotic memories; he has proceeded by means of a series of apostrophes to seek help from natural phenomena; gradually doubting his own musical ability and fearing that the fault may lie in him rather than in the sea, the moon, or the land, he has even considered his own technical performance; and since none of these shifts has restored his love, he now droops in despair: "O darkness! O in vain!"

Turning away from hope, he perceives that his singing "all the night" has been useless. He thus closes his song with a bittersweet passage (lines 125–129) in which he reminds himself again and for the last time of his joyful past, now quite hopelessly disconnected from present and future. His quest for completeness, a quest which the listening boy can identify with his own, has ended in failure because he is a bird, not a man. Because, unlike the boy, he is unable to entertain transcendental paradoxes, his despair is complete. Joys and pains he is unable to reconcile into a totality: they remain to him two entirely opposed experiences. In line 127 he reveals his incapacity to come to grips with his loss: the five-times repeated "Loved!" looks wholly backwards in time —it needs to be completed by what the sea, a voice of eternity instead of time, utters in the similar line 173: "Death, death, death, death, death." The bird is trapped in time, and his vision of experience, although undeniably pathetic, is partial, merely particular, and thus ultimately horrifying.

When the speaker resumes his narration in lines 130–143, he returns to participial syntax. The bird, silenced finally by a total hopelessness, has stopped singing, but the contextual sounds persist ironically. The bird's song now echoes emptily among the sounds of the wind's whistling, the sea's angry moaning, and the sand's gentle rustling. The moon is still sadly drooping, "the face of the sea almost touching." The phenomena of nature are not "touching" each other now: they are discrete, isolated, cold. And everything in nature is now either sad, or angry and fierce. But the listening boy is now, surprisingly, ecstatic. Possessed of the metaphor-making faculty denied the bird, the boy at this moment finds himself beloved by nature, which has not even noticed the bird's outcries. To the boy, the waves seem lovingly to dally with his bare feet; the air dallies with his hair—and the love in his heart, "long pent," responds. His ears and then his soul "swiftly depositing" the meaning not only of the bird's song but of nature's failure to attend to it, he weeps with joy as he begins to perceive his own paradoxical relationship with the bird. On the one hand, the bird is his "dusky demon and brother," his genius and his poetic type. And yet, on the other hand, the boy's essence transcends the bird's, for the boy is not obliged by his own nature to cease his quest at the point of despair: he can "translate" despair into joy, moving out of time into eternity.

He now speaks (line 140) of a "trio," the members of which, as in Italian opera, have each sung simultaneously different but related subjects. The first member of the trio is the sea, which, far from being troubled by loss, is herself a figure of infinite loss. The second member of the trio is the bird, troubled by loss but unable to regard loss in relation to a larger whole. The third member of the trio is the boy, who as an agent of perception—that is, a maker of metaphors—is as far removed from the bird as the bird is from the sea, even though the bird remains his "brother" and even though the sea stands as "mother" to both. The boy's recognition of his own nature here prompts him to perceive his identity and his function: "Now in a moment," he says, "I know what I am for." He awakes as if from a dream of darkness and feels starting up within him "a thousand warbling echoes" of the song of the bird.

The address of the speaker shifts suddenly in line 144, and from here to line 149 the boy (or rather his "soul") delivers his first apostrophe—his first extravagant metaphor—of the poem. He thus reveals that he has now learned to "echo" (but not, we should notice, to reproduce) bird-song; that is, to sing lyrically and as if instinctually. The speaker's customary "natural" mode of discourse, narrative recitative, now begins to take on qualities of the bird's mode, apostrophic aria. The boy has learned from the bird's long aria how to receive into his songs sorrow and loss and solitude (that is, "the sweet hell within") as central themes. But he has also learned something more—he has learned a rhetorical technique for managing such themes, as his new syntactical and rhetorical practice reveals. From this point onward the "out-setting bard" practices what he has learned from the bird's way of singing: the "unknown want, the destiny of me" (line 157) proves to be the fruition of a technique of address as well as an increased sense of personal coherence and a newly discovered poetic subject matter.

Lines 144–164 thus operate through apostrophe. After addressing the "Demon or bird" ("demon" in the sense of "spirit"), the speaker turns to address himself: "O solitary me listening, never more shall I cease perpetuating you." He then indulges in prophecy, and prophecy which, I think, has been sometimes misread:

> Never more shall I escape, never more the reverberations,
> Never more the cries of unsatisfied love be absent from me.

The speaker does not mean that he conceives of himself as a frustrated lover: we remember that, in the time-scheme of the past occasion, he is just a little boy. He means that he has discovered from the bird's song the way of rendering poetically (that is, through the device of "cries") the theme of unsatisfied love, taken as representative of a whole complex of themes accessible to the rhetorically sophisticated but quite inaccessible to "the peaceful child I was."

After the address to himself, ending in self-discovery and prophecy, the boy continues to exercise himself in his newly learned way of speaking. He apostrophizes the universe of natural appearances in general, seeking the "clew" which is still lurking in the night. Delighted with his success so far in extracting significance from natural particulars, the boy wants more; and what he wants now is one final "clew" which will lead him past the identity he has attained and which will carry him through to the goal of his quest: complete internal coherence within a completely coherent universe. Continuing (lines 160–162) to apostrophize the universe of natural particulars, the boy seeks one symbol which will serve as a "clew": "A word then, (for I will conquer it)." We may take the "it" here as referring to night as an emblem of obscurity and the absence of clear identity. And in lines 163–164 the boy moves on to perform the last apostrophe. He speaks now to the waves in a way which would have been impossible for him before learning from the bird the technique of addressing natural objects. He manages to ask of the waves the overwhelming question:

> Are you whispering it, and have been all the time, you sea
> waves?
> Is that it from your liquid rims and wet sands?

Like the bird, the boy has learned how to address the sea; the sea did not respond to the bird, for the bird, unaware that the sea was anything more than its "mere first sight," did not seek the "clew." But because the boy seeks (that is, employs his human metaphorical power), the sea, even though it is the alien element, condescends to answer:

> Whereto answering, the sea,
> Delaying not, hurrying not,
> Whisper'd me through the night, and very plainly before
> daybreak,
> Lisp'd to me the low and delicious word death.

And what is the knowledge of death a "clew" to? It is a clew to life and love, the end of the beginning which perpetually performs the completion of experience, uniting halves into wholes and thus providing a value higher than either life or death—the value, namely, resident in the conception of reality not as stasis but as process.

Line 170 reminds us of the "trio" in line 140, for it names the two other "singers" and distinguishes the sea from them: "Hissing melodious, neither like the bird nor like my arous'd child's heart." The sea neither hurries like the bird nor hesitates like the boy: reconciling a hiss with a melody, it is harmonious, coherent, complete. The boy's total immersion in his ecstatic awareness of coherent process is brilliantly imaged in lines 171–173, where the sea is depicted

> . . . edging near as privately for me rustling at my feet,
> Creeping thence steadily up to my ears and laving me softly all over.

The boy's new knowledge surrounds and sustains him the way water does a swimmer.

In the final section (lines 174–183), which marks a return from past to present, the reconciliation of the primary dualisms is insisted upon. It is a passage perhaps as stunning technically as any Whitman ever wrote; we will have to arrive at *Four Quartets* before we encounter in reflective American poetry anything so brilliant in meter, in figure, and in lithe idiomatic precision. Even the management of the assonance bespeaks the most sophisticated calculation. Almost regardless of our will we are borne through the passage by the echoing long *e* sounds which begin in "demon" (line 175) and proceed through "me," "beach," "key," "sweetest," "creeping," "sweet," "sea," and "me." The initial "which" refers both to the antecedent "death" and to the whole experience "in the moonlight on Paumanok's gray beach":

> Which I do not forget,
> But fuse the song of my dusky demon and brother,
>
> . . . .

With the thousand responsive songs at random,
My own songs awaked from that hour,
And with them the key, the word up from the waves,
The word of the sweetest song and all songs,
That strong and delicious word which, creeping to my feet,
(Or like some old crone rocking the cradle, swathed in sweet
    garments, bending aside,)
The sea whisper'd me.

The reconciliation between bird-song and man-song is fully effected by means of the "key"—the complete apprehension of death as a stage in organic process; this knowledge enables the human singer to transcend despair and to bring coherence into the apparently opposed conditions of life and death. As we are told in Section 45 of "Song of Myself,"

Every condition promulges not only itself, it promulges what
    grows after and out of itself,
And the dark hush promulges as much as any.

Although Whitman's curious warble is finished, the speaker is saying that nothing else ever is. The oppositions of joys and pains, ecstasy and despair, instinct and control, nature and art, are now ready to lie down together, each completing the other to bring forth a harmonious and satisfactory universe. At the end of the poem, the sea, imaged earlier as "the savage old mother" (line 141), has turned curiously benign: although she is undeniably old, indeed, eternal, she is now rocking an infant in its cradle, bending in her sweet garments, lisping and whispering now instead of moaning and crying. And this final figure, which Whitman added with consummate structural tact to the version of

1881, carries us back to the figure with which the poem began, the figure of the sea as itself an eternally rocking cradle. The final figure suggests the psychological reconciliation in the coherent person between his youth and his age: his cradled infancy and his maturity, his boyhood and his manhood, his innocence and his knowledge, have fused. Emerson defines "the lover of Nature" as "he whose inward and outward senses are still truly adjusted to each other; who has retained the spirit of infancy even into the era of manhood." And from this kind of internal coherence springs a vision of an analogous, corresponding universe of coherent externals. Inner process corresponds with outer. As we find asserted in "A Song of the Rolling Earth," "I swear the earth shall surely be complete to him or her who shall be complete." In a famous setting not entirely different from that of "Out of the Cradle," Arnold finds consolation, if not ecstasy, in the continuing possibility of private human fidelities; but the speaker in our poem sings his "Ah, love, let us be true to one another!" not, characteristically, to a woman in a room but both to the boy he once was and to the whole universe of external forms. It is, as Samuel Johnson said of his marriage, "a love match on both sides." Having constructed a psychologically coherent personal history, and having attained to a universe which he has made coherent, the speaker in the poem is now prepared to render his vision in coherent poetic forms, for, as we have seen, "aria" and "recitative," representative of two opposed kinds of expression, the poem finally reconciles in a sort of "ensemble."

Glancing back over the poem, we now can see that all things in it come in pairs: we have a sun and a moon, a he-bird and a she-bird, a boy and a man, south and north, sand and sea, darkness and light, past tense and present tense, shadows and substances, love and death. All partake at the end in the process of reconciliation, which resembles the process by which, in an individual metaphor, the two parts interpenetrate to create a third thing. The behavior of the poem thus resembles one vast metaphor in the process of becoming: the dual but multiform terms of the great figure that is the poem lock at the end to admit both speaker and reader into a new reality. The final revelation occurs significantly at the light-in-darkness of dawn, an image of the reconciliation of the light and darkness which have opposed each other earlier in the poem. Whitman's command to his dualistic details, a command which the details obey cheerfully, is a version of E. M. Forster's epigraph to *Howards End:* "Only connect." And the details obey cheerfully because Whitman has contrived them so that they will obey. He does not, that is, find them on the beaches of Long Island and then catalogue them. He makes them up. The "key" which the boy seeks and finds in the poem will not, I think, admit us into any of the dark, winding corridors of Whitman's actual life. But the key does do something perhaps even better. It unlocks both for Whitman and for us the front door of the palace of art.

Richard Chase

"OUT OF THE CRADLE"

AS A ROMANCE

I am not entirely happy with the word "romance" as applied to "Out of the Cradle Endlessly Rocking," but it is the best word I can think of for my purpose. I am sure its meaning will not be immediately clear. After all, "Out of the Cradle" is not a poem about sexual love and courtship; it is not a medieval allegory; it has no knights in shining armor and no chivalry to speak of. I use the word "romance" as I did in my book on the American novel,* to suggest certain literary qualities which are characteristically, though not exclusively, American, and to suggest, therefore, that Whitman's poem has certain things in common with the writings of Poe, Hawthorne, Melville, and others among our fictionists, beyond what has been noticed by such careful comparative critics as F. O. Matthiessen.

In keeping with my definition of American "romance" in my book on the novel, I use the term to suggest that "Out of the Cradle" is one of the many American works of literature whose chief moods are those of idyl and melodrama. I intend to suggest that the poem achieves its own finished form only by means of

* *The American Novel and Its Tradition* (New York, 1957).

disrupting into irreconcilable and extreme contradictions the universe of which it speaks. And I intend to suggest that although
the main question raised in the poem is nothing less complex and
interesting than the origin of the poet's genius, the answer the
poet gives us is too pat and strikes us as only a half truth, if a
truth at all. Finally, I intend to suggest that the world of moral
experience set forth in "Out of the Cradle" is a treacherous world
to live in. I had better hasten to add, though it may sound like a
paradox, that I think "Out of the Cradle" a great poem, and one
of Whitman's best. There is no reason why a master of his language should not transmute into poetic form some very dubious
materials, and Whitman has done this in "Out of the Cradle."
Even so, the poem falls short of the tragic utterance it tries to be
and remains somewhere in the second rank behind the world's
greatest poems. In doing so it aligns itself with many of the best
American poems and novels.

But before pursuing these matters further, let me set down
some notes toward a general view of Whitman. In *Democratic
Vistas* Whitman speaks of the need for a moral and spiritual re-
generation in America. He allots to the poet, or as he is oddly
called, the literatus, a highly important place. We are told the
main characteristics of the literatus and of the national literature
he will produce. The literatuses of the future, not too surprisingly,
will resemble Walt Whitman, or rather—and this is an important
distinction—they will resemble Whitman as he thought of himself in his public role as a prophet and teacher. The image of the
literatus *Democratic Vistas* projects is of a poet who furnishes
archetypes (Whitman's word) for an optimistic, "orbic," "kosmical" America, an America devoted to "a strong-fibred joyous-

ness and faith, and the sense of health *al fresco*." There is little enough here to remind us of the Whitman we have come in recent years to understand—the real Whitman, the divided, covert, musing, "double," furtive man, poet and showman, who wrote the poems we prize. These poems of course are by no means always orbic or kosmical. For neither Whitman himself nor his disciples ever quite succeeded in making him into the prophet or the teacher-philosopher. This is most fortunate, for otherwise we would have lost the Whitman who with his be-witching combination of ego and doubt, of charlatanism and sincerity, of comic self-regard and wistful nostalgia, of neurosis and health wrote poems such as "Song of Myself," "Crossing Brooklyn Ferry," and "As I Ebb'd with the Ocean of Life." "Our Walt Whitman," says Leslie Fiedler, "is the slyest of artif-icers . . . he is a player with illusion; his center is a pun on the self; his poetry is a continual shimmering on the surfaces of concealment and revelation that is at once pathetic and comical." Mr. Fiedler goes on to say that Whitman was not, or not in essence, the tribal bard. "He was only a man, ridden by impotence and anxiety, by desire and guilt, furtive and stubborn and half-educated. That he became the world's looked-for, ridicu-lous darling is astonishing enough; that he remained a poet through it all is scarcely credible." These words are from Mr. Fiedler's excellent essay called "Images of Walt Whitman."

For a further description of the poet who is here being called *"our* Walt Whitman," one might look into the pages of the first book really to understand this poet, Constance Rourke's *American Humor*. But there is also Randall Jarrell's essay en-titled "Some Lines from Whitman" (in his *Poetry and the Age*)

and my own book of 1955, *Walt Whitman Reconsidered*. If
these writings delineate "our Walt Whitman," why then is my
book, or at least the chapter on "Song of Myself," described by
Mr. Willard Thorp (in *Eight American Authors,* published by
MLA) as "to say the least, aberrant"? I would have been grateful
to Mr. Thorp if he had said "unorthodox" instead of "aberrant."
For there has indeed been an orthodoxy among most Whitman
scholars. It is not the orthodoxy of the original disciples and of
Edgar Lee Masters, that makes Whitman a messiah and tribal
bard. It is the orthodoxy of the history-of-ideas approach to
literature that makes Whitman a philosopher or possibly even
a theologian of the mystic variety (not that vain Walt wouldn't
have been pleased by the compliment). This approach is to be
found, for example, in James E. Miller's recent *A Critical Guide
to Leaves of Grass,* which, in taking Whitman for a religious
mystic, descends from such different works as Richard M. Bucke's
Cosmic Consciousness and Hart Crane's *The Bridge.* I would
think that the critical reader who embarks on a reading of Whitman, as Mr. Miller does, with a copy of Evelyn Underhill's
*Mysticism: A Study in the Nature and Development of Man's
Spiritual Consciousness* at hand, would do well to have also at
hand a copy of Tocqueville's *Democracy in America* and of Miss
Rourke's book mentioned above. I would think that instead of
looking for the Immortal and the Ineffable, the Cosmic and the
Mystical, he might look, as in his imperfect way Whitman looked,
at the realities of a democratic civilization.

   Or consider as another example of the purely intellectualist
approach, Gay Wilson Allen's *Walt Whitman Handbook.* With
all its talk of immanence and emanation, acosmism and cosmo-

theism, pantheism and panpsychism, the book never gets around
to a discussion of Whitman's real subject, which is the plight
and destiny of the self. It is impossible to sympathize with Mr.
Allen's contention that "an exhaustive comparative study needs
to be made of the relations of Whitman's thought to the [Great]
Chain of Being." Poor old Walt, he had never heard of the Great
Chain of Being. His leading conceptions are the self, equality,
and contradiction—appropriate preoccupations for the poet of
American democracy. What use had he, in a democratic culture,
for the philosophic counterpart of European hierarchies? Surely
we shall not take too seriously, although generations of scholars
have, Whitman's fancy references to Hegel, Plato, and other
philosophers.

But to return to the projected literatus of *Democratic Vistas,*
he resembles in one respect at least the deepest and most genuine
Whitman. Only people unfamiliar with Whitman's own poems
will be surprised when he remarks that "in the future of these
States must arise poets immenser far, and make great poems of
death." There are indeed many great poems of death in American
literature, both in verse and prose, although none of the authors
—Poe, Emily Dickinson, Melville, Stephen Crane, to mention a
few—resembles the literatus any more than does Whitman himself—I mean Whitman the genuine, the immortal poet. Among
these great poems of death belongs "Out of the Cradle Endlessly
Rocking."

Before we come to a closer examination of this poem, let us
consider its place in the Whitman canon. I am aware that my
idea of this is at odds with what is or for a long time was the
conventional view of Whitman's development. This view (and

I believe that in many academic halls it still is the conventional view) was well expressed in 1932 in an essay by Mr. Floyd Stovall called "Main Drifts in Whitman's Poetry." The Parringtonian title of Mr. Stovall's essay is not amiss, for he does not trace Whitman's development by looking at the poet and his poems in their sheer naked insistent quiddity. He traces it, as he himself says, by following the currents of Whitman's "thought." Since the older one is the more "thought" one has had a chance to acquire, it is a foregone conclusion that Whitman's writing, as it goes through its various stages, gets better and better. As Mr. Stovall sees it, we have three stages in Whitman's poetry. The first is characterized by "Song of Myself," with its brash but unthinking self-assertion and its unexamined optimism; in this first stage Whitman, though thirty-six when "Song of Myself" was published, is still "immature." The second stage is announced by "Out of the Cradle," a tragic love poem in which a sobered Whitman confronts death and gains a mature or whole view of life. "Death is the consoler," wrote Mr. Stovall, "the clue to man's destiny, because it is the divine complement of human imperfection through which love is made complete and immortal." (But where, one might ask, does the poem make love complete and immortal? It seems rather to say that love is unstable and without an object—unless indeed that object is death in and for itself, for death is not presented in this poem as the gateway to the immortal or as a compensatory term in the rhythm of life.) As I have said, "Out of the Cradle" does not strike me as a tragic poem, and people who call it that seem to use the word either in the ordinary but unsatisfactory sense, as referring to anything that is very sad, or in some vaguely honorific sense.

During the second stage, the argument continues, Whitman's "thought" waxed and deepened as he became less interested in the self and more interested in the community and the fate of mankind. In the third stage, characterized best by "Passage to India," Whitman grew more spiritual and conservative and aware of the divine, universal plan of things. As Mr. Stovall says, "Love, already national in scope, now reached out to include the entire world." I do not myself see why love reaching out to include the entire world should necessarily be regarded as a good thing. Diffuseness, whether of love or anything else, was always Whitman's Waterloo as a poet. And far from being a step forward, Whitman's gradually slackening sense of the self and its dialectical relations with the not-self, a slackening which we begin to observe in his work after the 1855 edition, was the beginning of the end of his greatness as a poet. The great poems of Whitman's middle period—"Out of the Cradle," "As I Ebb'd," "When Lilacs Last in the Dooryard Bloom'd"—are not an "advance" over "Song of Myself"; they are merely *different,* in style and tone. It would be just as true (that is, not true at all) to call them a "retreat" from "Song of Myself." Apart from their value as poetry, they seem really, in their elegiac mood, to constitute a kind of swan song, for although Whitman wrote much fine verse in later life his period of best accomplishment was surely between "Song of Myself" and "When Lilacs Last."

That "Out of the Cradle" is one of Whitman's best poems we do not need to spend much more time in affirming. Any sympathetic reader, not too encased in the Eliot-Pound tradition, must surely feel the magnificence of this poem, and I think this may be felt and admitted even by readers who, like myself, do not care for more cosmic and universalized utterances like "Salut au Monde" and "Passage to India." In those poems reality is diffuse and homogenized. In "Out of the Cradle" reality may be elusive, but once we have got hold of it, it is seen to be particular and concrete, besides having universal significance. Perhaps these qualities are what led Swinburne to call the poem "faultless" and "noble" and what inspired Henry James (as Edith Wharton tells us in an oft-quoted passage) to read aloud one evening from "Song of Myself" and then, his voice filling "the hushed room like an organ adagio," proceed to "the mysterious music of 'Out of the Cradle,' reading, or rather crooning in a mood of subdued ecstasy till the fivefold invocation to Death tolled out like the knocks in the opening bars of the Fifth Symphony."

Nor do we need to spend much time in discussing the outward form of the poem and its main theme. There appears to be general agreement that the poem is constructed rather like an opera. It has a clearly discernible overture, followed by passages of recitative and aria. One may note, however, that the finale by no means matches the overture in symphonic complexity, being comparatively muted and, despite the richly suggestive images of the bird, the sea, and the old crone rocking the cradle, relatively downright and matter of fact in tone. The conclusion is a short recessional rather than a finale.

The main theme of "Out of the Cradle," though it does not exhaust the meanings of the poem, is the origin of the poet's genius. Whitman asks for and receives from the sea a "clew" or "word," and we are led to understand that his poetic genius originated in childhood and its first intuition of the alienation and loss which are the lot of all beings and which culminate in death. "Out of the Cradle," then, is a poem about the origin of poetry and to this extent is similar to Yeats's "Byzantium" and certain books of Wordsworth's *Prelude*. If this is not clear from the poem itself, we have as guideposts the two earlier titles Whitman gave to it: "A Child's Reminiscence" and "A Word Out of the Sea."

Is Whitman right, by the way, in tracing the origin of his poetry as he does? At best he seems to be only half right, for the world of experience posited in "Out of the Cradle" is not that of "Song of Myself," a greater poem and in many ways more characteristic of the author.

What is not so clear is how much else, if anything, the poem means. Is it, as is often said, an "organic" poem, affirming a whole view of reality in which life and death or love and death are understood as compensatory parts of the living universal rhythm? Mr. Miller, in his chapter on "Out of the Cradle," thinks that it is this kind of poem and provides us with a good statement of his position. He is speaking about the conclusion of the poem:

> The sea waves, "delaying not, hurrying not," repeat their single word, "Death, death, death, death, death." The slow and funereal march of the stress ironically recalls the preceding lines of heavy, repeated stresses, lines of both joy and sorrow. The sea waves' line not only recalls but also reconciles or merges the joy with the sorrow, for the hypnotic effect ("Creeping thence steadily up to my ears and laving me softly all over") precipitates in the soul of the protagonist not terror but the ecstasy of mystic insight and affirmation. Something of the nature of that insight is sug-

gested parenthetically at the end of the poem. Those sea waves striking unceasingly and rhythmically against the shore, forming the spiritually fertile "liquid rims" are "like some old crone rocking the cradle." The poem ends as it began ("Out of the cradle endlessly rocking"), and the cycle of the experience, like the cycle of life, is begun again. Life and death are not the beginning and end, but rather ceaseless continuations. Death is birth into spiritual life. The sea, as it sends its waves unceasingly to the seashore, is the "cradle endlessly rocking," just as the spiritual world, through the mystic experience of death, provides the "cradle" for man's spiritual birth.

There are many things to be said about this passage. One might start with the language and politely desire of Mr. Miller that he eschew the word "protagonist" unless the sense of the Greek word is precisely demanded. A "protagonist" combats something, but what, in "Out of the Cradle," is the "protagonist" combating? It is actually the *poet* who speaks in this poem. Then there is that other word that seems often to go with "protagonist"—"insight," the insight we and the protagonist get when the protagonist has a confrontation with something. The insight Mr. Miller attributes to the protagonist is not really an insight; it is a highly abstract idea, for which there is no warrant in the poem. Finally the word "mystic"—"the ecstasy of mystic insight and affirmation" and "the mystic experience of death." I can conceive of a mystic insight, though I would want to call it an "intuition," but an affirmation is necessarily of the will and the mystic experience requires a suspension of the will. Nor do I think much is gained by saying that the experience of death in the poem is "mystic." It strikes me as being immediate and poignant; the poem would be poorer if it were not. In talking about poetry we are often tempted to use the word "mystic" in order to beg a question or to talk about something other than what we ought to be talking about: namely, the poem. I am not particularly interested in whether or not Whitman may be properly called a "mystic," because the question is so largely irrelevant to the poems. As I said in my book on Whitman:

> It seems a matter of general principle that poetic experience, although it may include it, cannot be equated with or produced by mystic experience, properly so called. Mysticism leads to the ecstatic contemplation of the naught; it does not of itself produce poetry, which is a metaphorical construction of the aught. Poetry is made by the imagination, and, as Santayana insists, the life of reason depends on our ability to distinguish between the imaginative and the mystic (although he himself failed to do so in his attack on Whitman). I do not wish to deny the usefulness of the word "mysticism" in speaking of the general tenor of Whitman's mind, but only to doubt its relevance to the strictly literary question and to the question of his emergence as a poet.

My general objection to Mr. Miller's formulation occurred to me when he passed confidently by the "old crone rocking the cradle." I don't feel comfortable with that "old crone" despite her "sweet garments" (shrouds can be "sweet") and despite her cradle-rocking activities. She gives me the creeps and I can't help feeling that at not too many levels of meaning below the surface that cradle is a coffin. It is certainly true that many of Whitman's poems—including some of his best, such as "Song of Myself"—affirm an organic universe and an immortal and universal rhythm of life, but "Out of the Cradle" is not one of them. The quality of experience conveyed by this poem—the experience out of which poetry is born—involves love without an object; it involves anxiety, alienation, insoluble contradiction, and ultimate despair, a despair not assuaged by the sentimental resignation with which it is embraced.

The illusion of a harmonious universe in which opposites or contradictions are reconciled is sustained only at the very beginning of the poem. There the "musical shuttle" out of "the mocking-bird's throat" draws into a unity that which is "down" and that which is "up":

> Down from the shower'd halo,
> Up from the mystic play of shadows twining and twisting as
>   if they were alive . . .

And at the beginning of the poem the poet can confidently speak of himself as the "chanter of pains and joys, uniter of here and hereafter." The feeling of reconciliation and harmony rises to an early pitch in the aria of the two birds:

> *Shine! Shine! Shine!*
> *Pour down your warmth, great sun!*
> *While we bask, we two together.*
> *Two together!*
> *Winds blow south, or winds blow north,*
> *Day come white, or night come black,*
> *Home, or rivers and mountains from home,*

> *Singing all time, minding no time,*
> *While we two keep together.*

But the illusion of unity and continuity is not sustained, or is
sustained only fitfully, after this aria. For now the she-bird has
suddenly disappeared, and the he-bird sings his melancholy dirge,
pouring out meanings, as Whitman cryptically says, "which I
of all men know." A reader mindful of Whitman's love of melodrama, of which he encountered aplenty in the Italian operas
he was so fond of, will find the first ominous note in this ominous
poem in the "surging of the sea," for this surging is described
as "hoarse," and although we may see nothing necessarily frightening in this at first, the context of the poem forces us to remember
that ghosts and other demonic creatures are often said to speak
with a hoarse and sepulchral voice. Even the "white arms out in
the breakers tirelessly tossing" which Whitman remembers seeing
during the childhood experience he is recapturing or re-creating
do not seem on reflection to be so attractive and winsome as
they do at first. There is something threatening, something beyond human control, something suggestive of a universe indifferent to human destiny, in that tireless tossing. Or perhaps there
is something merely suggestive of death, for the arms of a corpse
in the sea might toss tirelessly.

The object of love is now unattainable, though there is still the
compulsion to pursue it in panic and madness, a pursuit now seen
as an act of nature itself:

> *O madly the sea pushes upon the land,*
> *With love, with love.*

And whereas once the white and the black were held together in a unison,

> *Day come white, or night come black,*

they are now seen in an ultimate opposition:

> *What is that little black thing I see there in the white?*

The song of the he-bird now rises to a pitch of desperate assertion:

> *Shake out carols!*
> *Solitary here, the night's carols!*
> *Carols of lonesome love! death's carols!*
> *Carols under that lagging, yellow, waning moon!*
> *O under that moon where she droops almost down into the*
>   *sea!*
> *O reckless despairing carols.*

And finally the song recedes into a resigned reminiscence of what used to be: "We two together no more."

Although we now hear "the aria sinking," "all else" continues; the stars shine, the winds blow, the notes of the bird echo. But "all else" does not continue in a compensatory or organic harmony. Instead, the world has fallen apart. There is no object for "the love in the heart long pent" even though it is "now loose, now at last tumultuously bursting." This is a world characterized by loss and alienation, not presided over by a benign Great Mother, as Whitman of all poets might have wished, but haunted and agitated by the "angry moans" of "the fierce old mother incessantly moaning." Through the fissures of a disjoined world there enter the demonic powers always drawn upon by

the imagination of melodrama. Does the boy, the poet-to-be, receive comforting and joyous answers to his questions about his destiny? Far from it:

> The undertone, the savage old mother incessantly crying,
> To the boy's soul's questions sullenly timing, some drown'd
> secret hissing,
> To the outsetting bard.

At this point the bird is addressed as "demon or bird," and I think we are safe in taking "demon" in both of its usual meanings: the poetic genius and a sinister emanation from some unknown realm. The latter meaning is confirmed by the imagery that occurs a bit later, where the bird is called a messenger, as if from some infernal place:

> The messenger there arous'd, the fire, the sweet hell within,
> The unknown want, the destiny of me.

Perhaps it is also sustained by the later phrase "my dusky demon and brother." As I have already suggested, neither the fivefold invocation to death, the dusky demon, nor the old crone at the end of "Out of the Cradle" suggests a world stabilized in a compensatory order of life and death. If we have read the poem clearly we do not leave it confident that we live in a world of pain assuaged, contradictions reconciled, and disruptive powers placated, or that poetry originates in such a world. Despite its sentimentality, Whitman's poem is more clairvoyant and more extreme in its perception of disorder and dread than its critics have seen, although these same critics would readily discern the same qualities in the works of other American romancers, such as Cooper, Poe, Hawthorne, and Melville.

Let me recall at this point the fascination Whitman felt for Poe and his writings. As he tells us in *Specimen Days,* he thinks that Poe's verses "by final judgment, probably belong among the electric lights of imaginative literature, brilliant and dazzling, but with no heat." Nevertheless, he says, there is "an indescribable magnetism" about these poems with their "incorrigible propensity toward nocturnal themes" and their "demoniac undertone behind every page." And Whitman tells us that he had gradually lost his early distaste for Poe's writings. He then recounts a dream he had had about Poe: "I saw a vessel on the sea, at midnight, in a storm . . . flying uncontrolled with torn sails and broken spars through the wild sleet and winds and waves of the night. On the deck was a slender, slight, beautiful figure, a dim man apparently enjoying all the terror, the murk, and the dislocation of which he was the centre and the victim." That makes a good description of the author of "Out of the Cradle"—a dim man apparently enjoying all the terror, the murk, and the dislocation of which he was the center and the victim.

But, it might be asked, is not my account of "Out of the Cradle" at odds with the obvious feelings the poet means to leave us with? These feelings involve sadness, to be sure, but they seem to culminate, if not in happiness, then in resignation in the face of loss and unrequited love. And death itself, it might be argued, is not felt to be terrible; indeed it is embraced with a kind of tender eroticism, not to mention gustatory delight—"the low and delicious word death." It seems to me that the language of the poem sustains these feelings of resignation and benignity so well that it is all too easy to take them as the sum and substance of the poem. As D. H. Lawrence admonishes us, we must look below the surface of these American authors. When we look below the surface of "Out of the Cradle" we seem to see the dark workings-out of a human drama being played on a stage set by a dramatist with a dubious moral to propose, namely that we should accept death and that this acceptance may be the origin of such creations as Whitman's poetry. This would be excellent morality if the sense of it were: "Let us accept death as a fact, and let this fact thereby enhance our life." But Whitman does not say anything like this. He is titillated by death and he forms a sentimental attachment to it. The idyl of the two birds ends near the beginning of the poem, but the idyllic tone, modulated into a somber key, strangely continues. And in fact what the poet does is nothing less than endow the ominous drama of the savage old mother, the lagging moon, and the dusky demon with the emotional quality of an idyl; he thus successfully muffles and suffuses but cannot banish what is going on under the surface. The melodious words and the bland universe of experience make one level of the poem, but the submerged, disrupted, and ultimately nihilistic impulses remain active.

We do not have to be professional psychoanalysts in order to make the plausible conjecture that the reason for the disjunction between the manifest and the latent content of Whitman's poem is to be found in the poet's own emotional life. The generally accepted view of Whitman is that he was more or less bisexual, that he tended toward the homosexual, that he was perhaps not very active sexually at all, and that love, for him, was either fraternal or maternal—he was unable to endow a father image with emotional power or to convey, except in very abstract terms, the nature of heterosexual love. In "Out of the Cradle" the neurotic Whitman has it all his own way. There is no image of paternity: "fish-shaped" Paumonok is not identified with the father here, although it is in "As I Ebb'd with the Ocean of Life." The marriage of sexual equals is symbolically exorcised in the loss of the she-bird by the he-bird. The he-bird is not felt as a father, but as "my dusky demon and brother." In this world bereft of the father-principle, the mother is all-encompassing, like the sea. But what is the price the poet has to pay for his denial and extinction of the father? Well, of course, it is anxiety and ambivalence, involving both love and dread, toward the mother. Thus, it is not surprising that while the poet is enjoying with such swooning pleasure the rocking of the cradle, the mother supplying the motive power should be an "old crone" who "bends aside" and whispers hoarsely.

On the surface, in other words, the embracing of death is presented as pleasurable and as the beginning of creative acts. Beneath the surface it is recognized as an act of neurotic regression which generates powerful and sinister impulses that threaten the destruction of personality. This is why I speak of the "melodramatic" quality of "Out of the Cradle," apart from its obvious use of some of the trappings of this mode of art. Whitman's distinctive emotional nature is to be found in the conflicts of the unresolved Oedipus complex we all of us more or less live with (and it is here rather than in the sentimental invocation to death that we discover the real origins of Whitman's poetry—insofar as we discover them at all). Melodrama, like some forms of comedy—farce, for example—is precisely a drama of unresolved conflicts or contradictions.

The poem called "Tears" is a kind of footnote to the more lachrymose sections of "Out of the Cradle." This short lyric starts out as a rather impressive piece but at the end, where we read about "the unloosen'd ocean/ Of tears! tears! tears!" it is hard not to be reminded of Alice in Wonderland, swimming in the ocean she has made with her weeping. Nevertheless the ambiguity or doubleness of "Out of the Cradle" is well represented, and in a more literal way, in "Tears." Here the poet imagines himself to be "sedate and decorous by day, with calm countenance and regulated pace." But at night he is a ghost with a "muffled head" weeping desperately on the beach:

> O who is that ghost? that form in the dark, with tears?
> What shapeless lump is that, bent, crouch'd there on the sand?
> Streaming tears, sobbing tears, throes, choked with wild cries;
> O storm, embodied, rising, careering with swift steps along
>   the beach?
> O wild and dismal night storm, with wind . . .

There is nothing here about an "outsetting bard." There is only an undifferentiated horror and in a gothicized setting an almost total extinction of personality.

If I am right in assigning to "Out of the Cradle" such terms as romance, idyl, and melodrama, it cannot, as I have noted before, be also a tragic poem. It would be surprising indeed if a work of personal confession whose main emotions culminate, as we must see, in a sentimental nihilism should be also a tragic work. The poem does not work its way through its own inner contradictions, its *agon,* and then proceed, as does tragedy, to issue in a higher synthesis or harmony. The embracing of death is not accompanied by a purgated emotion, because the emotion is not won; it is, we cannot help feeling, merely held in reserve so that at the proper time the poet can fall back on it. It is an emotion all too easily come by, in other words a sentimental, though not a shallow, emotion. "Song of Myself" can hardly be called a tragedy either, but that poem strikes me as having more of the essential nature of tragic art than does "Out of the Cradle" —at least, "Song of Myself" has, in the correct sense of the word, a protagonist. "Out of the Cradle" is a much more unified work of art than Melville's *Pierre* (to venture a distant comparison); but it seems to me to be related to "Song of Myself" roughly as *Pierre*—also a work that begins in idyl and ends in melodrama —is related to *Moby-Dick*. After the great aggressive act of creating a superb work of art there follows, for aesthetic, moral, or psychological reasons we cannot quite define, the rather desperate act of neurotic self-exposure. The poet who in "Song of Myself" glorified in the amplitude of a many-faceted personality has come in the Sea-Drift poems to doubt the very possibility of personality. He has been led, for whatever reason, to wonder whether the glorious autonomous self has not now become (in the memorable words of Fredrik Schyberg) "only a chance bit of wreckage thrown up on the shore of existence."

The characteristic form of American fiction which I call in a special sense "romance" is one which defines itself by its substitution of two-dimensional figures, often allegorized, for the rounded characters who appear in the more ample form of the novel. It defines itself, that is, by a reduction of personality. For this reason, among the others I have pointed out, romance is a suitable form for "Out of the Cradle Endlessly Rocking."

Roy Harvey Pearce

WHITMAN JUSTIFIED:

THE POET IN 1860

> Where are we going, Walt Whitman? The doors close in an hour.
> Which way does your beard point tonight?
> Allen Ginsberg, "A Supermarket in California"

My title comes from the fourteenth of the "Chants Democratic"
in the 1860 *Leaves of Grass*. (This is the poem which finally
became "Poets to Come.") The first two stanzas read:

> Poets to come!
> Not to-day is to justify me, and Democracy, and what we
>   are for,
> But you, a new brood, native, athletic, continental, greater
>   than before known,
> You must justify me.
>
> Indeed, if it were not for you, what would I be?
> What is the little I have done, except to arouse you?

Whitman is, he concludes, "the bard" of a "future" for which he
writes only "one or two indicative words."

The vision is utopian, of course—and became increasingly so
in the 1870s and 1880s, when he was calling for, even guaranteeing,
a state of things whereby poems would work so as eventually to

make for the withering away of poetry. In a preface of 1872 he could claim:

> The people, especially the young men and women of America, must begin to learn that Religion, (like Poetry,) is something far, far different from what they supposed. It is, indeed, too important to the power and perpetuity of the New World to be consigned any longer to the churches, old or new, Catholic or Protestant—Saint this, or Saint that. . . . It must be consigned henceforth to Democracy *en masse,* and to Literature. It must enter into the Poems of the Nation. It must make the Nation.

And by 1888 (in "A Backward Glance O'er Travel'd Roads") he could claim that, contrary to European critical opinion, verse was not a dying technique.

> Only a firmer, vastly broader, new area begins to exist—nay, is already form'd—to which the poetic genius must emigrate. Whatever may have been the case in years gone by, the true use for the imaginative faculty of modern times is to give ultimate vivification to facts, to science, and to common lives, endowing them with glows and glories and final illustriousness which belongs to every real thing, and to real things only. Without that ultimate vivification—which the poet or other artist alone can give—reality would seem to be incomplete, and science, democracy, and life itself, finally in vain.

These two statements (and they are quite typical) sum up Whitman's growing sense of the power of poetry, and thus of the poet: Religion, operating as poetry—and *only* as poetry—can make the nation, vivify it: or, in the language of a late poem like "Passage to India," "eclaircise" it.

"In the prophetic literature of these states," he had written in 1871 (in *Democratic Vistas*), ". . . Nature, true Nature, and the true idea of Nature, long absent, must, above all, become fully restored, enlarged, and must furnish the pervading atmosphere to poems." And later in the same essay: "The poems of life are great, but there must be poems of the purports of life, not only in itself, but beyond itself." Life beyond life, poetry beyond poetry: this idea came to count for more and more in Whitman's conception of his vocation and, accordingly, of that of the poets who were to come. The last edition (1892) of *Leaves of Grass* is surely the testament of the sort of "divine literatus" whom he had earlier prophesied. Indeed, he had not only prophesied himself but made the prophecy come true. But, as he acknowledged, this was not the only form of his testament. For, when he wrote of the last edition, "I am determined to have the world know what *I* was pleased to do," he yet recognized: "In the long run the world will do as it pleases with the book." The question remains: How may we use the book so as to know what we please to do with it? And more: What does the book, in its structure and function, in its growth, teach us about the vocation of poet in the modern world? And more: How may it help the poets who yet are to come discover, and so define, their vocation?

The hard fact—so it seems to me—is that Whitman fails as prophetic poet, precisely because he was such a powerfully *humane* poet. The adjective makes us flinch, perhaps; but only because, like Whitman, we have found the beliefs it implies so difficult to hold to that we have come, if not to seek for the prophetic utterances which will offer us something in their stead, then to discount them as disruptive of the high sense of our private selves on which we ground our hopes for the lives we live. Still, it might be that a close reading of Whitman, the poet of 1860—for it is he whom I suggest we must recover—will teach us what it might be like once more to hold to them.

Be that as it may, the record of Whitman's life would suggest that his own power, his own humanity, was at the end too much for him. In any case, when he tried to write prophetic poetry, he came eventually to sacrifice man—that finite creature, locked in time and history, at once agonized and exalted by his humanity —for what he has encouraged some of his advocates again to call cosmic man—the cosmic man of, say, these lines from "Passage to India":

> Passage, immediate passage! the blood burns in my veins!
> Away O soul! hoist instantly the anchor!
> Cut the hawsers—haul out—shake every sail!
> Have we not stood here like trees in the ground long enough?
> Have we not grovel'd here long enough, eating and drinking
>   like mere brutes?
> Have we not darken'd and dazed ourselves with books long
>   enough?
>
> Sail forth—steer for the deep waters only,
> Reckless O soul, exploring, I with thee, and thou with me,
> For we are bound where mariner has not yet dared to go,
> And we will risk the ship, ourselves and all.

> O my brave soul!
> O farther farther sail!
> O daring joy, but safe! are they not all the seas of God?
> O farther, farther, farther sail!

It is the idea of that "daring joy, but safe"—everywhere in the poem—which prevents one from assenting to this passage and all that comes before it. The passage of a soul, whether it is everyman's or a saint's, is not "safe," however "joyful." So that Whitman cannot focus the poem on the sort of *human* experience to which one might assent, because one could acknowledge its essential humanity. The figures in the passage proliferate farther and farther out from whatever center in which they have originated, until one wonders if there ever was a center. Probably not, because the experience of the protagonist in this poem is that of cosmic man, who, because he is everywhere, is nowhere; who, because he can be everything, is nothing. *This* Whitman, I believe, is he who mistakes vivification for creation, the ecstasy of cadence for the ecstasy of belief, efficient cause for final cause, poet for prophet. Which is not, I emphasize, the same as conceiving of the poet *as* prophet.

Whitman's genius was such as to render him incapable of the kind of discipline of the imagination which would make for the genuine sort of prophetic poetry we find in, say, Blake and Yeats: of whom we *can* say that they were poets *as* prophets; for whom we can observe that poetry is the vehicle for prophecy, not its tenor. Whitman is at best, at *his* best, *visionary,* and sees beyond his world to what it might be—thus, what, failing to be, it is. Blake and Yeats are at best, at *their* best, *prophetic,* and see through their world to what it really is—thus, what, pretending not to be, it might be. Visionary poetry projects a world which the poet would teach us to learn to acknowledge as our own; it comes to have the uncanniness of the terribly familiar. Prophetic poetry projects a world which the poet would teach us is alien to our own yet central to our seeing it as it really is—a world built upon truths we have hoped in vain to forget. We say of the visionary world that we could have made it—at least in dream-work. We say of the prophetic world that we could not possibly have made it, for it was there already. The ground of visionary poetry is indeed dream-work and magical thought; the ground of prophetic poetry, revelation and mythical thought. Thus the special language of prophetic poetry—one of its most marked formal characteristics—must, by the definition of its purpose, be foreign to us (for it reveals a world, and the strange things in it, hidden from us); yet, by the paradox of prophecy, it is a language native to us (for the things it reveals, being universal—out of the realm of day-to-day time, space, and conception—put all of us, all of our "actual" world, under their aegis). We can "understand" that language because its grammar and syntax are analogous to our own; understanding it, we assent to—and perhaps believe in—the metaphysical system which its structure and vocabulary entail; trying to account for its origin, we agree with the poet that he has been, in some quite literal sense, "inspired."

Now, when the mood came over him—as it did increasingly—perhaps Whitman did claim to have been "inspired" in this literal sense. But even so, his later work fails as prophetic poetry (for that is what it is meant to be) precisely because, like the earlier work, it projects not a world to which the poet stands as witness but one to which he stands as maker. Yet he asks of the world projected in the later work that, in accordance with the requirements of prophetic poetry, it have the effect of revelation; that its language be at once of and not of our workaday world; that it imply what in *Democratic Vistas* he called a "New World metaphysics." Yet the editions of *Leaves of Grass* from 1867 on fail of the centrality and integrity of properly prophetic poetry: fail, I think, because the poet mistakenly assumes that poetry, when it is made to deal with the universe at large, *becomes* prophecy. For all his revisions and manipulations of his text, for all his enlargement of his themes, the later Whitman is but a visionary poet. And, since he asks more of it than it can properly yield, the vision, and consequently the poetry, even the conception of the poet, get increasingly tenuous. A certain strength is there, of course. But it is the strength of an earlier Whitman, who perhaps prophesied, but could not bring about, his own metamorphosis from poet to prophet. His genius was too great to let him forget that, after all, it was *poets* who were to come.

True enough, he wrote, toward the end of "A Backward Glance O'er Travel'd Roads":

> But it is not on "Leaves of Grass" distinctively as *literature,* or a specimen thereof, that I feel to dwell, or advance claims. No one will get at my verses who insists upon viewing them as a literary performance, or attempt at such performance, or as aiming mainly toward art or aestheticism.

One says: How right, how sad, how wasteful! For, ironically enough, Whitman's words characterize the *failure* of the 1892 *Leaves of Grass.* And one turns to the earlier Whitman, I daresay the authentic Whitman, whose verses did aim mainly toward art and aestheticism: toward a definition of the vocation of the poet in that part of the modern world which was the United States.

For me, then, the most important edition of *Leaves of Grass* is the 1860 edition; and its most important poem is "A Word Out of the Sea" (which, of course, became "Out of the Cradle Endlessly Rocking" in later editions). Here Whitman may be best justified: as a poet. The burden of this paper will be to justify Whitman's way with poetry in the 1860 volume; to show how the structure and movement of this volume and of some of the principal poems in it (above all, "A Word Out of the Sea") are such as to furnish a valid and integral way for a poet dedicated to saving poetry for the modern world, thus—as poet, and only as poet—dedicated to saving the modern world for poetry. The Whitman of the 1860 *Leaves of Grass* would be a sage, a seer, a sayer. But he speaks of only what he knows directly and he asks of his speech only that it report fully and honestly and frankly, only that it evoke other speeches, other poems, of its kind. The poems in this volume do justify Whitman's claims for poetry in general—but in terms of what he may in fact give us, not of what he would like, or even need, to give us. The strength of the major poems in the volume is that they some-how resist *our* need for more than they present, and make us rest satisfied—or as satisfied as we ever can be—with what they give. Above all, this is true of "A Word Out of the Sea"—as it is less true, and so less characteristic, of the later Whitman, the poet of "Out of the Cradle Endlessly Rocking."

The 1855, 1856, and 1860 *Leaves of Grass* make a complete sequence—one in which the poet invents modern poetry, explores its possibility as an instrument for studying the world at large and himself as somehow vitally constitutive of it, and comes finally to define, expound, and exemplify the poet's vocation in the modern world. The sequence, in brief, is from language to argument; and it is controlled at all points by a powerful sense of the ego which is struggling to move from language to argument and which must come to realize the limits of its own humanity, which are the limits of argument. If, as we well know, the poet as envisaged in the 1855 and 1856 *Leaves of Grass* is the counterpart of him of whom Emerson wrote in "The Poet" (1844), the poet envisaged in the 1860 *Leaves of Grass* is the counterpart of him of whom Emerson wrote in his essay on Goethe in *Representative Men* (1850): Not Shakespeare, not Plato, not Swedenborg would do for the modern world, which yet "wants its poet-priest, a reconciler." Goethe was one such: "the writer, or secretary, who is to report the doings of the miraculous spirit of life that everywhere throbs and works. His office is a reception of the facts into the mind, and then a selection of the eminent and characteristic experiences." Note: just a "writer" (what John Holloway in an important book of a few years ago called the *Victorian Sage:* a philosopher of a kind, but one who constructs his argument according to a grammar of assent). Emerson had concluded:

> The world is young: the former great men call to us affectionately. We too must write Bibles, to unite again the heavens and the earthly world. The secret of genius is to suffer no fiction to exist for us; to realize all that we know; in the

high refinement of modern life, in arts, in sciences, in books, in men, to exact good faith, reality and a purpose; and first, last, midst and without end, to honor every truth by use.

The 1860 *Leaves of Grass,* as one of Whitman's notebook entries indicates, was to be a Bible too: "The Great Construction of the New Bible. . . . It ought to be ready in 1859." It was to offer a "third religion," Whitman wrote. And in a way it does; but, for well and for ill, that religion is a religion of man—man as he is, locked in his humanity and needing a religion, yet not claiming to have it by virtue of needing it; not hypnotizing himself into declaring that he has it. (For Whitman a little cadence was a dangerous, if exciting, thing, much cadence, disastrous.) The Whitman of the 1860 *Leaves of Grass* is, par excellence, Emerson's "secretary," reporting "the doings of the miraculous spirit of life that everywhere throbs and works." To accept a miracle, to live in its presence, even to try to comprehend it—this is not the same as trying to work one, even claiming to have worked one. And—as the poets who have come after him have variously testified in their puzzled, ambiguous relation to him—Whitman's way with the language of poetry, going against the grain of mass communications and "positivism," may well teach us how to recognize and acknowledge miracles. It cannot teach us how to work them; or even how to earn them. One can well imagine how hard it must be for a poet to go so far with language, only to discover that he can go no farther. Such a discovery constitutes the principal element of greatness in the 1860 *Leaves of Grass,* perhaps the principal element of greatness in Whitman's poetry as a whole.

I have said that in 1855 Whitman "invented" modern poetry. By this I mean only that, along with other major poets of the middle of the century, he participated—but in a strangely isolated way—in the development of romanticist poetics toward and beyond its symbolist phase. ("To invent" may mean, among other things, "to stumble upon.") I do not mean to claim too much for the word "symbolist" here; I use it only generally to indicate that Whitman too came to realize that a poet's vocation was fatefully tied to the state of the language which constituted his medium. He discovered with Baudelaire—although without Baudelaire's (and incidentally Emerson's) overwhelming sense of the problem of "correspondences"—that, as regards language, "tout vit, tout agit, tout se correspond." The medium thus had a "life" of its own, and so might generate "life"—the "life" of poetry. Poetry, in this view, thus became *sui generis,* a unique mode of discourse; and the role of the poet became more and more explicitly to be that of the creator: one who might "free" language to "mean"—a creator in a medium, pure and simple.

We have in Whitman's early work a version of that conception of poet and poetry with which we are now so familiar: To whom was the poet responsible? Not to whom, the reply ran, but to what? And the answer: to language. And language as such was seen to be the sole, overriding means to establish, or reestablish, community. The perhaps inevitable drift—not only in Whitman's work but in that of his contemporaries and of the poets who have come—was toward an idea of poetry as a means of communion, perhaps modern man's sole means of communion, his religion. Professor Abrams (in *The Mirror and the Lamp*) concludes his account of these developments thus:

> It was only in the early Victorian period, when all discourse
> was explicitly or tacitly thrown into the two exhaustive modes
> of imaginative and rational, expressive and assertive, that
> religion fell together with poetry in opposition to science,
> and that religion, as a consequence, was converted into poetry,
> and poetry into a kind of religion.

Professor Abrams is speaking about developments in England.
In the United States, conditions were somewhat simpler and,
withal, more extreme. From the beginning, that is to say, Whitman was sure that the imaginative and rational might well be
subsumed under a "higher" category, which was poetry. So that
—as I have indicated in my remarks on Whitman and prophetic
poetry—for him there was eventually entailed the idea that the
New Bible might be just that, a total and inclusive account of
cosmic man, of man as one of an infinitude of gods bound up in
Nature. It is a nice question whether or not the "symbolist" dedi-
cation to the idea of language-as-communion must *inevitably*
lead to a search for a metalinguistic structure of analogies and
correspondences and then to an idea of poetry as religion and
religion as poetry. And it is a nicer question whether or not
"symbolist" poetics—with its emphasis on medium as against
matrix, language per se as against language-in-culture—is characterized by a certain weakness in linguistic theory. Whitman's
work raises these questions; and a full critique of his work would
entail a critique of his theory of poetry, thus of his theory of
language, thus of his theory of culture. But this is not the place
to speak of critics to come, much less to prophesy them.

In any case, we must grant Whitman his special kind of "unmediated vision." But we are not by that token obliged to grant, or claim for, him a "mysticism"—or, for that matter, "an inverted mysticism"; or to declare that, *ecce,* his poetry is at once *"mystical and irreligious";* or to see in the Whitman of 1855 a good, (prematurely) grey *guru.* (I cite here the recent claims for this Whitman of James Miller, Karl Shapiro, and Malcolm Cowley, who confuse, or conflate, this poet with the one who presided at Camden. And I think of the question, put with such sweet craziness, by Allen Ginsberg in the line I have used as epigraph.) At its most telling, Whitman's earlier poetry manifests what has been called (by Erich Kahler) an "existential consciousness," but of a mid-nineteenth-century American sort—its key term, its center of strength and weakness, being not anguish but joy. Or rather, the key term is triumph—as, suffering, the poet endures and rejoices: seeing that it is his vocation as poet to teach men that they can endure. The freedom which ensues is wonderful, not dreadful.

Thus I take the 1855 and 1856 editions of *Leaves of Grass,* which most freshly project this mode of consciousness, as stages on the way to the 1860 edition. In 1855 and 1856 Whitman shows that he has learned to report truthfully what he has seen; in 1860, that he has learned to measure its significance for the poet taken as the "secretary"—the archetypal man. He strove to go beyond this, but in vain. The movement from the 1855 to the 1856 editions is the movement from the first "Song of Myself" and the first "The Sleepers" (both originally untitled) to the first "Crossing Brooklyn Ferry" (called, in 1856, "Sun-Down Poem") : the poet first learns to discipline himself into regressing deeply into his own pre-conscious; then, with his new-found sense of himself as at once subject and object in his world, he learns to conceive in a new way of the world at large; he is, as though for the first time, "in" the world. The crucial factor is a restoration of the poet's vital relationship to language. A good, powerfully naive account of this discovery is that in Whitman's prose *American Primer,* written in the 1850s but not published until after his death:

> What do you think words are? Do you think words are positive and original things in themselves? No: Words are not original and arbitrary in themselves.—Words are a result —they are the progeny of what has been or is in vogue.—If iron architecture comes in vogue, as it seems to be coming, words are wanted to stand for all about iron architecture, for all the work it causes, for the different branches of work and of the workman.
>
> . . . .
>
> A perfect user of words uses things—they exude in power and beauty from him—miracles in his hands—miracles from his mouth.
>
> . . . .
>
> A perfect writer would make words sing, dance, do the male and female act, bear children, weep, bleed, rage, stab, steal, fire cannon, steer ships, sack cities, charge with cavalry or infantry, or do any thing, that man or woman or the natural powers can do. [Note the insistence on "natural," not "supernatural," powers.]
>
> . . . .
>
> Likely there are other words wanted.—Of words wanted, the matter is summed up in this: when the time comes for

them to represent any thing or state of things, the words will
surely follow. The lack of any words, I say again, is as historical as the existence of words. As for me, I feel a hundred
realities, clearly determined in me, that words are not yet
formed to represent.

These sentiments generally, and some of these phrasings particularly, got into Whitman's prose meditations. More important,
from the beginning they inform the poems. They derive much
from Emerson's "The Poet," of course; but they are not tied to
even Emerson's modestly transcendental balloon. The power
which Whitman discovers is the power of language, fueled by
the imagination, to break through the categories of time, space,
and matter and to "vivify" (a word, as I have said, he used late
in his life—so close to Pound's "make it new") the persons,
places, and things of his world, and so make them available to
his readers. In the process—since the readers would, as it were,
be using words for the first time—he would make them available
to themselves: as poets in spite of themselves.

It is as regards this last claim—that the reader is a poet in spite
of himself—that the 1860 *Leaves of Grass* is all-important. For
there Whitman most clearly saw that the poet's power to break
through the limiting categories of day-to-day existence is just
that: a poet's power, obtaining only insofar as the poem obtains,
and limited as the poem is limited. In 1860, that is to say, Whitman saw that his Bible was to be a poet's Bible, and had to be
built around a conception of the poet's life: his origins, experience, and end; his relation with the persons, places, and things
of his world. The 1855 and 1856 *Leaves of Grass* volumes are but
collections of poems—their organization as rushed and chaotic as

is the sensibility of the writer of the *American Primer*. *Within* individual poems, there is form, a form which centers on the moment in the poet's life which they project. But the 1860 *Leaves of Grass* is an articulated whole, with an *argument*. The argument is that of the poet's life as it furnishes a beginning, middle, and end to an account of his vocation. The 1860 volume is, for all its imperfections, one of the great works in that romantic mode, the autobiography. Or, let us give the genre to which it belongs a more specific name: archetypal autobiography. The 1860 volume is autobiographical as, say, *Moby-Dick* and *Walden* are autobiographical; for its hero is a man in the process of writing a book, of writing himself, of making himself, of discovering that the powers of the self are the stronger for being limited. The hero who can say No! in thunder discovers that he can say Yes! in thunder too—but that the thunderation is his own and no one else's.

Now, to say that the 1860 *Leaves of Grass* is quintessentially autobiographical is to say what has been said before, most notably by Schyberg, Asselineau, and Allen. But I mean to say it somewhat differently than they do. For they see in the volume a sign of a crisis in Whitman's personal life; and this is most likely so. Yet I think it is wrong to read the volume as, in this *literal* sense, personal—that is, "private." (The Bowers edition of the surviving MS of the 1860 edition clearly shows that Whitman —naturally enough, most often in the "Calamus" poems— wanted to keep the book clear of too insistently and privately personal allusions. He was, I think, not trying to "conceal"—much less "mask"—his private personality but to transmute it into an archetypal personality. I think that it is a mistake to look so hard, as some critics do, for the "private" I.) Thus I should read the volume as not a personal but an archetypal autobiography: yet another version of that compulsively-brought-forth nineteenth-century poem which dealt with the growth of the poet's mind. (Well instructed by our forebears, we now have a variety of names for the form—all demonstrating how deeply, and from what a variety of nonliterary perspectives, we have had to deal with the issues which it raises for us: *rite de passage,* quest for identity, search for community, and the like.) Whitman's problem, the poet's problem, was to show that integral to the poet's vocation was his life cycle; that the poet, having discovered his gifts, might now use them to discover the relevance of his life, his *lived* life, his *Erlebnis,* his *career,* to the lives of his fellows. It is the fact that his newly discovered use of poetry is grounded in his sense of a life lived-through: it is this fact that evidences Whitman's ability here, more than in any version of *Leaves of Grass,* to contain his gift and use it, rather than be used by it. Of *this* volume Whitman said: "I am satisfied with *Leaves of Grass,* (by far the most of it) as expressing what was intended, namely, to express by sharp-cut self assertion, One's Self & also, or may be still more, to map out, to throw together for American use, a gigantic embryo or skeleton of Personality, —fit for the West, for native models." Later, of course, he wanted more. But he never had the means beyond those in the 1860 edition to get what he wanted. And that has made all the difference.

The 1860 *Leaves of Grass* opens with "Proto-Leaf" (later, much revised, as "Starting from Paumanok"). Here Whitman announces his themes and, as he had done before, calls for his new religion; but he gives no indication that it is to be a religion of anything else but the poet's universalized vocation. (My misuse of the word "religion" is his. I mean neither to be victimized nor saved by following him here.) It might yet, on this account, be a precursor to a religion, in the more usual (and I think proper) sense, as well as a substitute for it. "Whoever you are! to you endless announcements," he says. There follows "Walt Whitman," a somewhat modified version of the 1855 poem which became "Song of Myself." It is still close to the fluid version of 1855; strangely enough, it is so overarticulated (with some 372 sections) that it does not have the rather massive, and therefore relatively dogmatic, articulation of the final version. In all, it gives us an account of the poet's overwhelming discovery of his native powers. Then in the numbered (but not separately titled) series of poems called "Chants Democratic," the poet—after an apostrophic salutation to his fellows (it ends "O poets to come, I depend on you!")—celebrates himself again, but now as he conceives of himself in the act of celebrating his world. The chief among these poems—as usual, much modified later—became "By Blue Ontario's Shore," "Song of the Broad-Axe," "Song for Occupations," "Me Imperturbe," "I Was Looking a Long While," and "I Hear America Singing." Following upon "Walt Whitman," the "Chants Democratic" sequence successfully establishes the dialectical tension between the poet and his world—the tension being sustained as one is made to realize again and again that out of the discovery of his power for "making words do the male and female act" in "Walt Whitman" has come his power to "vivify" his world in the "Chants Democratic."

The transition to "Leaves of Grass," the next sequence—again

the poems are numbered, but not separately titled—is natural
and necessary. For the poet now asks what it is to make poems
in the language which has been precipitated out of the com-
munal experience of his age. The mood throughout is one of
a mixture of hope and doubt, and at the end it reaches a certitude
strengthened by a sense of the very limitations which initially
gave rise to the doubt. The first poem opens—and I shall presently
say more about this—with two lines expressing doubt; later—
when the prophetic Whitman couldn't conceive of doubting—
these lines were dropped in the poem, which became "As I
Ebb'd with the Ocean of Life." The second poem is a version of
an 1855 poem, "Great Are the Myths"; it was finally rejected
by Whitman as being, one guesses, too certain in its rejection
of the mythic mode toward which he later found himself aspiring.
The third poem, which, combined with the sixth, later became
"Song of the Answerer," opens up the issue of communication
as such. The fourth, a version of an 1856 poem which eventually
became "This Compost," conceives of poetry as a kind of naturalistic resurrection. It moves from "Something startles me
where I thought I was safest"—that is, in the poet's relation to
the materials of poetry—to a simple acknowledgment at the end
that the earth "gives such divine materials to men, and accepts
such leavings from them at last." The fifth (later "Song of Prudence") considers the insight central to the poet's vocation. To
the categories of "time, space, reality," the poet would add that
of "prudence," which teaches that the "consummations" of
poetry are such as to envisage the necessary relationship of all
other "consummations": the imagination's law of the conserva-

tion of energy. The sixth (which, as I have said, later became part of "Song of the Answerer") develops an aspect of the theme of the fourth and fifth; but now that theme is interpreted as it is bound up in the problem of language: "The words of poems give you more than poems,/ They give you to form for yourself poems, religions, politics, war, peace, behavior, histories, essays, romances, and everything else." At this depth of discovery there is no possibility of any kind of logically continuous catalogue of what words "give you to form for yourself." Poetry is a means of exhausting man's powers to know the world, and himself in it, as it is. Beyond this, poems

> . . . prepare for death—yet they are not the finish, but rather the onset,
> They bring none to his or her terminus, or to be content and full;
> Whom they take, they take into space, to behold the birth of stars, to learn one of the meanings,
> To launch off with absolute faith—to sweep through the ceaseless rings, and never to be quiet again.

In the seventh poem (later "Faith Poem"), the poet discovers that he "needs no assurances"; for he is (as he says in the eighth poem, later "Miracles") a "realist" and for him the real (by which he means *realia*) constitutes "miracles." The poet is led, in the ninth poem (later "There Was a Child Went Forth"), to a recollection of his first discovery of the miraculousness of the real, a discovery he only now understands; this poem, taken in relation to the rest of the sequence, properly anticipates "A Word Out of the

Sea." The tenth poem opens, in a passage dropped from the later version, "Myself and Mine"—but one which is essential as a transition in the sequence:

> It is ended—I dally no more,
> After today I inure myself to run, leap, swim, wrestle, fight . . .

Simply enough: the poet, having accepted his vocation and its constraints, is now free—free *through* it; and he must now teach this freedom to others:

> I charge that there be no theory or school founded out of me,
> I charge you to leave all free, as I have left all free.

The rest of the sequence, some fourteen more poems, celebrates aspects of the poet's new freedom as it might be the freedom of all men. (I forebear giving their later titles.) It is the freedom to rejoice in the miraculousness of the real, and has its own costs. The greatest is a terrible passivity, as though in order to achieve his freedom, man had to offer himself up as the victim of his own newly vivified sensibility. Being as he is, the poet sees (in 12) "the vast similitude [which] interlocks all"; yet he must admit (in 15) "that life cannot exhibit all to me" and "that I am to wait for what will be exhibited by death." He is (in 17) the man who must "sit and look out upon all the sorrows of the world, and upon all oppression and shame"; and he must "See, hear, [be] silent," only then to speak. He declares (in 20): ". . . whether I continue beyond this book, to maturity/ . . . / Depends . . . upon you/ . . . you, contemporary America." Poem 24, wherein the poet completes his archetypal act, and gives himself over to his readers, reads:

Lift me close to your face till I whisper,
What you are holding is in reality no book, nor part of a book,
It is a man, flushed and full-blooded—it is I—*So long!*
We must separate—Here! take from my lips this kiss,
Whoever you are, I give it especially to you;
So long—and I hope we shall meet again.

I quote this last poem entire because I want to make it clear
that the lapses into desperate sentimentality—and this poem is
a prime example—are intrinsically a part of Whitman's autobiographical mode in the 1860 *Leaves of Grass,* as they are of the
mode, or genre, which they represent. It will not do to explain
them away by putting them in a larger context, or considering
them somehow as masked verses—evidences of Whitman the
shape-shifter. (Speaking through a *persona,* the poet perforce
hides behind it.) Confronting the agonies and ambiguities of his
conception of the poet, Whitman too often fell into bathos or
sentimentalism. Yet bathos and sentimentalism, I would suggest,
are but unsuccessful means—to be set against evidence of successful means—of solving the archetypal autobiographer's central
problem: at once being himself and seeing himself; of bearing
witness to his own deeds. If what he is, as he sees it, is too much
to bear; if he is incapable of bearing it; if his genius is such
as not to have prepared him to bear it—why then, his miraculism
will fail him precisely because he cannot stand too much reality.

Bathos and sentimentalism—and also anxious, premonitory
yearnings for something beyond mere poetry—inevitably mar
the rest of the 1860 *Leaves of Grass:* but not fatally, since they
are the by-products of its total argument. At some point, most

foxes want to be hedgehogs. Whitman is a poet who must be read at large. And I am claiming that Whitman can be best read at large in the 1860 *Leaves of Grass*. When he can be read in smaller compass—as in "A Word Out of the Sea"—it is because in a single poem he manages to recapitulate in little what he was developing at large. I should guess—as I shall presently try to show—that the large poem, the 1860 volume, is a necessary setting for the little poem, "A Word Out of the Sea." That poem (later, I remind my reader, "Out of the Cradle") is one of Whitman's greatest. And I shall want to show that it is even greater than we think. So I must carry through, however cursorily, my glance o'er the 1860 *Leaves of Grass*. There comes next a series of poems ("A Word Out of the Sea" is one of them) in which the poet meditates the sheer givenness of the world his poems reveal; he is even capable of seeing himself as one of the givens. But then he must specify in detail the nature of his kind of givenness: which includes the power to give, to bring the given to a new life. Here—after "Salut au Monde," "Poem of Joys," "A Word Out of the Sea," "A Leaf of Faces," and "Europe"—there is first the "Enfans d'Adam" sequence; and then, after an interlude of generally celebrative poems, the "Calamus" sequence. I want to say of these two sequences only that they are passionate in a curiously objective fashion; I have suggested that the proper word for their mood and tone is neither personal nor impersonal but archetypal. In context, they furnish analogues—directly libidinal analogues, as it were—for the poet's role, seen now not (as in the earlier sequences) from the point of view of a man telling us how he has discovered his gift, put it to use, and measured the cost of using it properly; but seen rather from the point of view of the reader. The "I" of these poems, I suggest, is meant to include the reader—as at once potential poet and reader of poems. So that the "Enfans d'Adam" sequence tells us how it is—what it means, what it costs—to be a maker of poems and the "Calamus" sequence how it is to be a reader of poems—in the first instance the analogue is procreation; in the second it is community. And if Whitman's own homosexuality led him to write more powerfully in the second vein than in the first, we should be mindful of the fact that, in his times as in ours, it seems to be easier to make poems, good poems, even to publish them, than to get readers for them.

Indeed, Whitman announces in the next-to-last of the "Calamus" sequence that we are to be ready for his most "baffling" words, which come in the last poem of the sequence, later "Full of Life Now":

When you read these, I, that was visible, am become invisible;
Now it is you, compact, visible, realizing my poems, seeking me,
Fancying how happy you were, if I could be with you, and become your lover;
Be it as if I were with you. Be not too certain but I am with you now.

Later Whitman changed "lover" to "comrade"—mistakenly, I think; for, as their function in the 1860 volume shows, the "Calamus" poems were to carry through to completion the poet's conception of his painfully loving relation with his readers.

Having, in the "Enfans d'Adam" and "Calamus" sequences, defined the poetic process itself, as he had earlier defined the poet's discovery of that process, Whitman proceeds variously to celebrate himself and his readers at once under the aegis of the "Enfans d'Adam" and the "Calamus" analogue. (As Lorca said in his "Oda," "Este es el mundo, amigo. . . .") Much of the power of the poems, new and old, derives from their place in the sequences. In "Crossing Brooklyn Ferry" and the series of "Messenger Leaves" there are addresses to all and sundry who inhabit Whitman's world, assurances to them that now he can love them for what they are, because now he knows them for what they are. There is then an address to Mannahatta—which returns to the problem of naming, but now with an assurance that the problem has disappeared in the solving: "I was asking for something specific and perfect for my city, and behold! here is the aboriginal name!" Then there is an address in "Kosmos" to the simple, separate persons—to each of his readers who is "constructing the house of himself or herself." Then there is "Sleep Chasings" (a version of the 1855 "The Sleepers"), now a sublime poem, in which the poet can freely acknowledge that the source of his strength is in the relation of his night-life to his daytime life, the unconscious to the conscious:

> I will stop only a time with the night, and rise betimes
> I will duly pass the day, O my mother, and duly return to you.

And "Sleep Chasings" is the more telling for being followed by "Burial" (an 1855 poem which eventually became "To Think of Time"). For in his incessant moving between night and day, the poet manages to make poems and so proves immortal. He makes men immortal in his poems, as he teaches them to make themselves immortal in their acts:

To think that you and I did not see, feel, think, nor bear
    our part!
To think that we are now here, and bear our part!

This poem comes virtually at the end of the 1860 volume. Only
an address to his soul—immortal, but in a strictly "poetic" sense
—and "So Long!" follow. In the latter we are reminded once
again:

This is no book,
Who touches this book, touches a man,
(Is it night? Are we alone?)
It is I you hold, and who holds you,
I spring from the pages into your arms—decease calls me
    forth.

We are reminded thus, to paraphrase a recent Whitmanian, that
in the flesh of art we are immortal: which is a commonplace.
We are reminded also that in our age, the role of art, of poetry,
is to keep us alive enough to be capable of this kind of immortality: which is not quite a commonplace.

The central terms in the argument of the 1860 *Leaves of Grass,*
I suggest, run something like this: first, in the poems which lead
up to "A Word Out of the Sea"—self-discovery, self-love, rebirth,
diffusion-of-self, art; and second, in the poems which follow "A
Word Out of the Sea"—love-of-others, death, rebirth, reintegra-
tion-of-self, art, immortality. The sequence is that of an ordinary
life, extraordinarily lived through; the claims are strictly human-
istic. The child manages somehow to achieve adulthood; the
movement is from a poetry of diffusion to a poetry of integration.

Immortality is the *result* of art, not its origin, nor its cause. The humanism is painful, because one of its crucial elements (centering on "death" as a "clew" in "A Word Out of the Sea") is an acknowledgment of all-too-human limitations and constraints. So long as Whitman lived with that acknowledgment, lived *in* that acknowledgment—even when living with it drove him (as it too often did) toward bathos and sentimentalism—he managed to be a poet, a "secretary," a "sage," a seer, a visionary. His religion was the religion of humanity: the only religion that a work of art can *directly* express, whatever other religion it may confront and acknowledge. *Indirectly,* it *can* confront religion in the more usual and more proper sense; for it can treat of man in his aspiration for something beyond manhood, even if it cannot claim— since its materials are ineluctably those of manhood—to treat directly of that something-beyond. The burden—someone has called it the burden of incertitude; Keats called it "negative capability"—is a hard one to bear. Whitman, I am suggesting, bore it most successfully, bore it most successfully for us, in the 1860 *Leaves of Grass*.

Which brings me to the most important of the poems first collected in this volume, "A Word Out of the Sea." It was originally published separately in 1859 as "A Child's Reminiscence." Thus far I have tried to suggest the proper context in which the poem should be read: as part of the volume for which it was originally written; as a turning point in the argument of that book. Note that "A Word Out of the Sea" comes about midway in the book after "Walt Whitman," the "Chants Democratic," "Leaves of Grass," "Salut au Monde," and "Poem of Joys"—that is, after those poems which tell us of the poet's discovery of his powers as poet and of his ability to use those powers so to "vivify" his world, and himself in it: after his discovery that it is man's special delight and his special agony to be at once the subject and object of his meditations; after his discovery that consciousness inevitably entails self-consciousness and a sense of the strengths and weaknesses of self-consciousness. Moreover, "A Word Out of the Sea" comes shortly before the "Enfans d'Adam" and "Calamus" sequences—that is, shortly before those poems which work out the dialectic of the subject-object relationship under the analogue of the sexuality of man as creator of his world and of persons, places, and things as its creatures. I cannot but think that Whitman knew what he was doing when he placed "A Word Out of the Sea" thus. For he was obligated, in all his autobiographical honesty, to treat directly of man's fallibilities as well as his powers, to try to discover the binding relationship between fallibilities and powers: to estimate the capacity of man to be himself and the cost he would have to pay. The poems which come before "A Word Out of the Sea" have little to do with fallibilities; they develop the central terms of the whole argument only this far: self-discovery, self-love, rebirth, art. Theirs is the polymorph perverse world of the child. In them, death only threatens, does not promise; power is what counts. The turning point in the poet's life can come only with the "adult" sense of love and death, the beginning and the end of things: out of which issues art, now a mode of immortality. In "A Word Out of the Sea" the 1860 volume has its turning point. Beyond this poem, we must remember, are the "Enfans d'Adam" and "Calamus" sequences, and "Crossing Brooklyn Ferry" and the "Messenger Leaves" sequence.

The 1860 poem begins harshly: "Out of the rocked cradle." The past participle, unlike the present participle in the later versions, implies no agent for the rocking; the sea here is too inclusive to be a symbol; it is just a fact of life—life's factuality. Then comes the melange of elements associated with the "sea." They are among the realities whose miraculousness the poet is on his way to understanding. Note the third line (omitted in later versions) which clearly establishes the autobiographical tone and makes the boy at once the product of nature at large and a particular nature: "Out of the boy's mother's womb, and from the nipples of her breasts." All this leads to a clear split in point of view, so that we know that the poet-as-adult is making a poem which will be his means to understanding a childhood experience. Initially we are told of the range of experiences out of which this poem comes: the sea as rocked cradle seems at once literally (to the boy) and metaphorically (to the poet) to "contain" the song of the bird, the boy's mother, the place, the time, the memory of the brother, and the as yet unnamed "word stronger and more delicious than any" which marks a limit to the meaning of the whole.

This is quite explicitly an introduction. For what follows is given a separate title, "Reminiscence," as though the poet wanted to make quite plain the division between his sense of himself as child and as adult. Then we are presented with the story of the birds, the loss of the beloved, and the song sung (as only *now* the poet knows it) to objectify this loss, so make it bearable, so assure that it can, in *this* life, be transcended. Always we are aware that the poet-as-adult, the creative center of the poem, seeks that "word stronger and more delicious" which will be his means

finally to understand his reminiscences and—in the context of
this volume (I emphasize: in the context of *this* volume)—serve
to define his vocation as poet: at once powerful and fallible. The
points of view of bird, child, and adult are kept separate until
the passage which reads:

> Bird! (then said the boy's Soul)
> Is it indeed toward your mate you sing? or is it mostly to me?
> For I that was a child, my tongue's use sleeping,
> Now that I have heard you,
> Now in a moment I know what I am for—I awake,
> And already a thousand singers—a thousand songs, clearer,
>   louder, more sorrowful than yours,
> A thousand warbling echoes have started to life within me,
> Never to die.

The boy, even as a man recalling his boyhood, does not, as in
later versions, at first address the bird as "Demon." He is at
this stage incapable of that "or"—in the later reading "Demon
or bird." Even though his soul speaks, he is to discover—some
lines later—his special "poetic" relation to the bird. Moreover,
as "boy," he holds toward death an attitude halfway between that
of the bird—who is merely "instinctive"—and that of the man
—who is "reflective," capable of "reminiscence." Yet the points
of view begin to be hypnotically merged—*after* the fact. In the
boy's "soul" the poet discovers a child's potentiality for adult
knowledge; but he keeps it as a potentiality, and he never assigns
it to the bird, who (or which) is an occasion merely. Yet having
seen that potentiality as such, he can "now," in the adult present,
work toward its realization, confident that the one will follow

necessarily in due course from the other. Now, in the adult present, he can ask for "the clew," "The word final, superior to all," the word which "now" he can "conquer." I cannot emphasize too much that it is a "word"—that the poet is translating the sea (and all it embodies) as pre-linguistic fact into a word, knowledge of which will signify his coming to maturity. "Out of," in the original title, is meant quite literally to indicate a linguistic transformation. In the record of the growth of his mind, he sees *now* that the word will once and for all precipitate the meaning he has willed himself to create, and in the creating to discover. And it comes as he recalls that time when the sea, manifesting the rhythm of life and death itself,

> Delaying not, hurrying not,
> Whispered me through the night, and very plainly before
>   daybreak,
> Lisped to me constantly the low and delicious word Death,
> And again Death—ever Death, Death, Death

(Not "Death," repeated four times as in later versions, but "ever," beyond counting. The prophetic Whitman was bound to drop that "ever," since for him nothing was beyond counting.)

The merging of the points of view occurs as not only past and present, child and adult, but subject and object (i.e., "The sea . . . whispered me"—not *"to* me") are fused. The poet now knows the word, because he has contrived a situation in which he can control its use; he has discovered (to recall the language of the *American Primer* notes) another reality, one that words until *now* had not been formed to represent. He has, as only a poet can, *made* a word out of the sea—for the duration of the poem understood "sea" as it may be translated into "death"—"ever death." His genius is such as to have enabled us to put those quotation marks around the word—guided by him, to have "bracketed" this portion of our experience with language; and we discover that as language binds us in the poet's time, so it is bound in human time.

If the end of the poem is to understand cosmic process as a continual loss of the beloved through death and a consequent gain of death-in-life and life-in-death—if this is the end of the poem, nonetheless it is gained through a creative act, an assertion of life in the face of death, and a discovery and acknowledgment of the limits of such an assertion. And this act is that of the very person, the poet, whom death would deprive of all that is beloved in life. Moreover, the deprivation is quite literally that and shows the poet moving, in high honesty, from the "Enfans d'Adam" sequence to "Calamus." In the 1860 volume, "A Word Out of the Sea" entails the "Calamus" sequence. (What if Whitman had, in "A Word Out of the Sea," written "comrade" instead of "brother"?)

In any case, at this stage of his career, Whitman would not yield to his longing for such comfort as would scant the facts of life and death. There is, I repeat, that opening "rocked," not "rocking" cradle; there is the quite naturalistic acknowledgment of the "boy's mother's womb." And there is stanza 31 (the stanzas in the 1860 poem are numbered, as the stanzas of the final version are not):

> O give me some clew!
> O if I am to have so much, let me have more!
> O a word! O what is my destination?
> O I fear it is henceforth chaos!

> O how joys, dreads, convolutions, human shapes, and all
> shapes, spring as from graves around me!
> O phantoms! you cover all the land, and all the sea!
> O I cannot see in the dimness whether you smile or frown
> upon me;
> O vapor, a look, a word! O well-beloved!
> O you dear women's and men's phantoms!

In the final version, the equivalent stanza reads only:

> O give me the clew (it lurks in the night here somewhere,)
> O if I am to have so much, let me have more!

The difference between "some clew" and "the clew" marks the difference between a poet for whom questions are real and one for whom questions are rhetorical. The later Whitman was convinced that the lurking clew would find him—and to that degree, whatever else he was, was not a poet. The earlier Whitman, in all humility, feared that what might issue out of this experience was "phantoms"—a good enough word for aborted poems. And often—but not too often—he was right.

Finally, there is not in "A Word Out of the Sea" the falsely (and, in the context of the poem, illogically) comforting note of "Or like some old crone rocking the cradle, swathed in sweet garments, bending aside." Indeed, the sentimentality and bathos of this too-much celebrated line, as I think, is given away by the fact that it is the only simile, the only "like" clause, in the poem. And, in relation to the total effect of the poem, the strategic withdrawal of the "Or" which introduces the line is at least unfortunate, at most disastrous.

I make so much of the kind of disaster, as I think it is, because

it became increasingly characteristic of Whitman's way with
poetry after the 1860 *Leaves of Grass.* Probably there are poems,
written later, which show him at his best; and probably some of
his revisions and rejections are for the best. But I more and more
doubt it, as I doubt that he had reached his best in 1855 and
1856. I do not mean to take the part of Cassandra; but I think it
as inadvisable to take the part of Pollyanna. The facts, as I see
them, show that Whitman, for whatever reason, after 1860
moved away from the mode of archetypal autobiography toward
that of prophecy. He worked hard to make, as he said, a cathedral
out of *Leaves of Grass.* He broke up the beautifully wrought
sequence of the 1860 volume; so that, even when he let poems
stand unrevised, they appear in contexts which take from them
their life-giving mixture of tentativeness and assurance, of
aspiration, and render them dogmatic, tendentious, and over-
weening.

In Lawrence's word, Whitman "mentalized" his poems. To
give a few examples of "mentalizing" revisions of 1860 poems:
the opening of the third "Enfans d'Adam" poem reads in the
1860 text:

> O my children! O mates!
> O the bodies of you, and of all men and women, engirth me,
>   and I engirth them.

In the 1867 version the lines read:

> I sing the body electric,
> The armies of those I love engirth me and I engirth them.

Another example: the opening line of the fourteenth poem of
the same sequence reads in the 1860 version: "I am he that aches

with love"; and becomes in 1867: "I am he that aches with amorous love." (This is the "amorous" which so infuriated Lawrence.) And another example: the opening lines of the fifteenth poem in the sequence read in the 1860 version: "Early in the morning,/ Walking . . ."; and become in 1867: "As Adam early in the morning,/ Walking. . . ." Small examples surely. But note the unsupported and unsupportable claims of "body electric," "armies," "amorous," and the Old Testament "Adam."

A larger—but still characteristic—example is Whitman's revision of the first of the 1860 "Leaves of Grass" sequence, which became "As I Ebb'd with the Ocean of Life." The 1860 poem opens thus:

> Elemental drifts!
> O I wish I could impress others as you and the waves have just been impressing me.
>
> As I ebbed with an ebb of the ocean of life,
> As I wended the shores I know.

In the poem as it appears in the 1892 edition of *Leaves of Grass,* the first two lines—expressing doubt, as I have pointed out—are missing; the third has been simplified to "As I ebb'd with the ocean of life"—so that the poet is no longer conceived as part of an "ebb." And the fourth line stands as we have it now. Later in the seventh line of the 1892 version, the poet says that he is "held by the electric self out of the pride of which I utter poems." In the 1860 version he says that he is "Alone, held by the eternal self of me that threatens to get the better of me, and stifle me." And so it goes—all passion beyond spending (unless vivified by

a kind of cosmic electroshock), all poetry beyond the mere writing, all life beyond the mere living—since the poet's tactic, however unconscious, is to claim to have transcended that which must
have been hard to live with: his extraordinarily ordinary self
and the ordinarily extraordinary death that awaits him. Granting
the mood and movement of the later editions of *Leaves of Grass,*
it is only proper that Whitman would have rejected the eighth
poem in the 1860 "Calamus" sequence, which begins "Long I
thought that knowledge alone would suffice me—O if I could but
obtain knowledge!" and ends, as the poet is brought to confront
the readers to whom he would offer his poems, "I am indifferent
to my own songs—I will go with him I love. . . ."

One more example: this one not of a revision but of an addition
to a sequence originating in the 1860 volume. In the 1871 *Leaves
of Grass,* Whitman, now wholly committed to making of his
poem a series of prophetic books, placed in the "Calamus"
sequence the woolly "Base of All Metaphysics," the last stanza
of which reads:

> Having studied the new and antique, the Greek and Ger-
>   manic systems,
> Kant having studied and stated, Fichte and Schelling and
>   Hegel,
> Stated the lore of Plato, and Socrates greater than Plato,
> And greater than Socrates sought and stated, Christ divine
>   having studied long,
> I see reminiscent to-day those Greek and Germanic systems,
> See the philosophies of all, Christian churches and tenets see,
> Yet underneath Socrates clearly see, and underneath Christ
>   the divine I see,

> The dear love of man for his comrade, the attraction of friend
>   to friend,
> Of the well-married husband and wife, of children and
>   parents,
> Of city for city and land for land.

Whitman stuck by this poem until the end, and it went unchanged into the 1892 edition of *Leaves of Grass,* contributing its bit to the "mentalizing" of the whole. And it is only too typical of additions to the book made from 1867 on.

This Whitman begins to take over *Leaves of Grass* in the 1867 edition and is fully in command by the time of the 1871 edition. It is, unhappily, he whom we know best and he with whom our poets have tried to make their pacts and truces—but, as I think, so that during the uneasy peace they might come to know another (and, as I have tried to show, earlier) Whitman: whose way with the poetry they seem to sense but can never quite get to. The way to that Whitman is not impassable, although working with the Inclusive Edition of *Leaves of Grass* (upon whose variant readings I have depended) is tedious. But there is yet a more direct way: reading the 1860 *Leaves of Grass.*

Meantime we must bring ourselves to say of the Whitman of 1892, the literatus, that he was driven to claim prophetic powers, not to put poetry to their service. Nothing could hold this Whitman back, not even the facts of a poet's life. Indeed, life—his own and life in general—became less "factual," less "real" for him. And—since justification consists in deriving the necessary from the real, of tracing the necessary back to its roots in the real, of showing that the real is necessary—he no longer had a need to justify himself. Well: In this our world, where we too find it increasingly hard to assent to the factually real, where we have got so far as to call the factually real the "absurd," we find it increasingly difficult to hold ourselves back: as do our poets, acting on our behalf. Thus I daresay we need to recover the Whitman of 1860—with his heroic sense of grounding the necessary in the real. He gave us permission to. I am suggesting that we *need* the poet of 1860, the poet of "A Word Out of the Sea." I mean to say thereby that our poets need him too. And justifying the need, we must justify him who contrived that his need be archetypal for ours.

Samuel Hynes

WHITMAN, POUND, AND THE

PROSE TRADITION

Every theory of poetry is a defense of poetry; every poet in his theorizing deals with, because he must deal with, the question, "What is your poem good for?" Among modern poets, there have been two principal answers to this question: either poetry supplies "the satisfactions of belief," or it provides a peculiar knowledge of the world's particulars. The first answer (which is Wallace Stevens's) leads us toward religion, or at least toward a surrogate for religion in the mystery and magic of *words;* the second (which is William Carlos Williams's) often seems to be a surrogate for science, and offers us the quiddities of *things.* Neither answer in itself provides an altogether adequate definition of the poetic act, and neither exactly describes any decent poet's practice; but together they do define the principal strategies by which modern poets have reasserted the authority of poetry, and preserved it from the abrogations of art-for-art's-sake. As such, it is important that they should be recognized and properly distinguished from each other.

One of the conventions of American literary history is that these two theoretical traditions have their American origins in the radical differences between Poe and Whitman: Poe, who defined "the poetry of words" as "the rhythmical creation of beauty," is regarded as the father of the "magical," symbolist tradition; Whitman, who wrote that "the true use for the imaginative faculty of modern times is to give ultimate vivification to facts, to science, and to common lives," is the patriarch of the poetry of things. Whitman himself, in his remarks on Poe, contributed to the establishment of the antithesis, and it has seemed true enough, and useful enough, to be preserved as a basic critical assumption.

Like most theories which divide complicated materials into two heaps, this one is an oversimplification. It is particularly unjust to Whitman, in that it seems to suggest that he was not interested in the verbal aspect of his medium; one need only remind oneself that *Leaves of Grass* was a "language experiment" to see that this is not true.

Nevertheless, it is true that poetic theory of the last hundred years has divided (if only roughly) into two traditions, and that the essential difference between them has been a difference in assumptions made about the essential nature of poetic reality. It also seems to me true that Whitman's principal influence on later American poets (and specifically, as I shall try to show, on the work of Ezra Pound) has been through his role of "poet of things."

We may get at the essence of the first tradition by recalling that conversation between Degas and Mallarmé in which Degas complained that he had plenty of ideas but couldn't finish his sonnet, and Mallarmé replied that poems are not made out of ideas but out of words. The conversation is memorable because Mallarmé's answer contains the core of an important modern theory, the theory that the essence of a poem—what the aestheticians call its ontological existence—is linguistic, and constitutes a world of imaginative experience distinct from ordinary existence. This is, of course, a principle of the Symbolists, but it has entered generally into the way we think about poetry.

We may approach the other tradition through another conversation, this one between Ezra Pound and T. E. Hulme. Pound's version of the exchange goes like this: "I spoke to him [Hulme] one day of the difference between Guido's precise interpretive metaphor, and the Petrarchan fustian and ornament, pointing out that Guido thought in accurate terms; that the phrases correspond to definite sensations undergone. . . . Hulme took some time over it in silence, and then finally said: 'That is very interesting'; and after a pause: 'That is more interesting than anything anyone ever said to me. It is more interesting than anything I ever read in a book.'"

I don't suppose any reader will find Pound's remark more interesting than anything he ever read in a book. And I don't really think Hulme found it so, either—the anecdote seems a clear case of the American innocent having his leg pulled. But the point that *is* interesting is that Pound thought his idea of precise phrases corresponding to definite sensations both valuable and original—valuable and original enough, in fact, to build a theory of poetry on. The theory that he constructed began, as Mallarmé's did, with a desire to purify the language of the tribe and to restore poetry to a place of value in human experience; but Pound moved in a direction opposite to the symbolist's. While Mallarmé put his faith in words, Pound committed himself more and more to the principle that ultimate reality lies in *things,* and that the essential poetic act must therefore be an exact rendering of things. This theory he called "the prose tradition," acknowledging thus his debt to Flaubert and realist aesthetics.

The phrase "prose tradition" first occurs in Pound's writings just before the First World War, and his most elaborate definitions of the tradition are from the same period. But there is nothing in his later work which contradicts, or even alters significantly, those early statements; Pound's poetic theory was fixed by the time he was thirty, and his theoretical remarks in the *Money Pamphlets,* the later *Cantos,* and the *Letters* merely repeat what he had said before. His most important statements date from the years 1913–16—the years immediately preceding the first *Cantos.* In the prose writings of this period we can see the process by which Pound formulated the aesthetic which underlies his epic; and it seems reasonable to say that the aesthetic had to be defined before the major work could proceed.

Pound introduced the phrase "prose tradition" in a sentence in one of his "Approach to Paris" essays in the *New Age* in 1913. Because this is the most detailed as well as the first statement of his theory, it is worth quoting at some length. Pound has been discussing a French poet called Laurent Tailhade, comparing him to Heine and Gautier. He continues:

> I think this sort of clear presentation is of the noblest traditions of our craft. . . . It is what may be called the "prose tradition" of poetry, and by this I mean that it is a practice of speech common to good prose and to good verse alike. It is to modern verse what the method of Flaubert is to modern prose, and by that I do not mean that it is not equally common to the best work of the ancients. It means

constatation of fact. It presents. It does not comment. It is irrefutable because it does not present a personal predilection for any particular fraction of the truth. It is as communicative as Nature. It is as uncommunicative as Nature. It is not a criticism of life, I mean it does not deal in opinions. It washes its hands of theories. It does not attempt to justify anybody's ways to anybody or anything else. . . . It is open to all facts and to all impressions. . . .

The presentative method does not attempt to "array the ox with trappings." It does not attempt to give dignity to that which is without dignity, which last is "rhetoric," that is, an attempt to make important the unimportant, to make more important the less important. . . .

The presentative method is equity. It is powerless to make the noble seem ignoble. It fights for a sane valuation.

Most of the familiar Poundian attitudes are here—the emphasis on plain speech and the presentation of facts, the anti-rhetorical bias, the hostility to didacticism and to personality in poetry (with a passing shot at his favorite antagonist, "the donkey-eared Milton"). It may not be all quite as Flaubert would have put it, but Pound is not far off when he says that he is applying Flaubert's methods to poetry.

It is not surprising, then, that Pound selected Ford Madox Hueffer as the occasion for his next "prose tradition" essay, "Mr. Hueffer and the Prose Tradition in English Verse." Hueffer was the most vocal disciple of Flaubert writing in England at the time, and from him Pound got a good deal of his aesthetic theory and some of his favorite aphorisms (it was Hueffer who first remarked that poetry should be written at least as well as prose). As a poet Hueffer was at best a minor talent, better than F. S. Flint, perhaps, and not quite as good as Aldington. Nevertheless, he was for Pound a "significant and revolutionary" poet, because Pound could see in Hueffer's *Collected Poems* what he was looking for, an "insistence upon clarity and precision, upon the prose tradition; in brief, upon efficient writing—even in verse."

He could also see that the prose tradition of which he had (rather inaccurately) made Hueffer the representative figure was antithetical to another current mode of poetry, the kind represented by Yeats; that is to say, he recognized in 1913 the two directions in which modern poetry was moving. "Mr. Hueffer's beliefs about the art," Pound wrote then,

> may be best explained by saying that they are in diametric opposition to those of Mr. Yeats. Mr. Yeats has been subjective; believes in the glamour and associations which hang near the words. "Works of art beget works of art." He has much in common with the French symbolists. Mr. Hueffer believes in an exact rendering of things. He would strip words of all "association" for the sake of getting a precise meaning. He professes to prefer prose to verse. You would find his origins in Gautier or in Flaubert. He is objective.

Not only did Pound recognize the two traditions; he also saw the poetic dangers implicit in each—that the prose tradition "tends to lapse into description," while the symbolist "tends to lapse into sentiment." But between description and sentiment, the former was obviously the lesser sin. Pound felt, as most of his contemporaries did, that sentiment had dominated English verse of the past century, and that it had dulled the tools of poetry with vague emotionalism, high-minded moralizing, and rhetorical decoration. The role that Pound set for himself was to resharpen poetry's cutting edge.

The strategies by which Pound set about this resharpening process are familiar enough to students of modern poetry: the "Few Don'ts by an Imagiste"; the note on Imagism written by Flint, but at Pound's dictation, for *Poetry;* the anthologies—*Des Imagistes* and the *Catholic Anthology;* Vorticism; the publicizing of Fenollosa's work. What these propaganda moves had in common was a theory of language, which Pound put most succinctly in a letter to Harriet Monroe: "language is made of concrete things." Imagism starts here; *The Cantos* start here, on this concrete foundation.

In the general tenor of his linguistic theory Pound is not, of course, by any means unique; his mistrust of the conventional cognitive properties of language is characteristic of a great deal of twentieth-century thought. A kind of "neonominalism" is part of the intellectual climate of our time. Numerous literary and philosophical examples come to mind: J. Alfred Prufrock, who find it impossible to say just what he means; Frederick Henry, who will not use words like *honor* and *courage* because they have been made meaningless; Stephen Daedalus and Leopold Bloom conversing without communicating in the cabman's shelter. The theme of failure of communication, the preoccupation with inarticulateness, are part of the same pattern, and so are some of the most quoted remarks of our literary heroes: the objective correlative, "no ideas but in things," "It was before all to make you see," "Dramatize! Only dramatize!" This emphasis on the

physical and the nondiscursive, this direct and immediate appeal
to sensory response, is so much a part of what we call modern
literature that words like *didactic,* and even *intellectual,* have become terms of opprobrium when applied to imaginative writing.
A similar mistrust is evident in much of twentieth-century philosophy—in logical positivism, in general semantics, in the current
Oxford school, in Ogden and Richards, in Wittgenstein. (I suppose one might argue that it has its correlative also in nonrepre-
sentational painting.)

But if Pound's nominalism has been in a main current of
his time, he has gone further with it than most of his contemporaries have. Starting with the Flaubertian ideals of economy,
precision, and objectivity, he took a further theoretical step which
separated him ontologically from his source—he argued the idea
of an exact rendering of *things* with a literalness which language
cannot sustain. Pound's letters to Iris Barry in 1916 are the most
detailed record of this conclusion, although, typically, the theoretical points are squeezed in between reading lists, comments
on literary reputations, and gossip. Here is a passage from a letter
of July 27, 1916; as usual, Pound has been drawing up reading
lists for the education of the young.

> Shifting from Stendhal to Flaubert suddenly you will see
> how much better Flaubert writes. AND YET there is a lot in
> Stendhal, a sort of solidity which Flaubert hasn't. A trust
> in the thing more than the word. Which is the solid basis,
> i.e. the thing is the basis.

Now how can this be made to make sense? How *can* a writer,
whose medium is necessarily words, put his trust in *things?* Per-

haps by carrying a sack of things around on his back, like the pro-
jector in *Gulliver's Travels*, but surely not in any more reasonable
way. The quoted passage assumes that to the question "What is
literature made of?" there are two possible answers—*words* and
things—and that these answers are absolute and antithetical. But
it should be obvious to the most casual consideration that *both*
answers are right. Poems are of course made of words—what
else? But since words are referential, poems can also be said
to be made of the referents of their words—of Penelopes, Flau-
berts, obstinate isles, and Muses' diadems. No contradiction is
involved in asserting that both statements are true. We may, of
course, say that poems with more exact sensory referents are
better poems, but this doesn't seem to be what Pound is saying.

Pound goes farther out on his limb in another passage in the
same letter:

> The whole of art is divided into:
> *a.* concision, or style, or saying what you mean in the
> fewest and clearest words.
> *b.* the actual necessity for creating or constructing some-
> thing; of presenting an image, or enough images of con-
> crete things arranged to stir the reader.
> Beyond these concrete objects named, one can make simple
> emotional statements of fact, such as "I am tired," or simple
> credos like "After death there comes no other calamity."
> I think there must be more, predominantly more, objects
> than statements and conclusions, which latter are purely op-
> tional, not essential, often superfluous and therefore bad.

This strikes me as an extraordinary statement for a poet to make.
As advice to a young girl writing poetry in 1916 it no doubt had

its practical value; but still, the size of the baby that Pound throws out with the bath is startling.

There are two antitheses implied in the quotation: words vs. things, and general words vs. particular, concrete words. The first is specious, as I have already argued; poems are both words and things. The second is perfectly legitimate, so long as it is not confused with the first. But Pound does confuse the two here, in order to suggest that there is a greater degree of reality, a closer relation to the actual, in words which name concrete objects than there is in "credos." He does so by using words like *construct, concrete, object, things*—words which suggest a more than verbal existence in the poetic creation. Perhaps he draws back slightly from this extreme position when he allows that his concrete objects are in fact only *named* (names are, after all, as abstract as credos), but the general impression he gives is that things are only "called by their right names" when they are presented in images. The passage, taken as a whole, is a fallacious argument for a poetry of things, by which the discursive efficacy of words is minimized, and poems become relationships among arranged objects—or rather, perhaps, among the images of objects.

When Pound identifies imagery with the naming of concrete objects, he exposes one of the weakest and most crucial points in his whole theoretical position. It is curious, but true, that though Pound is generally regarded as the Prime Minister of Imagism, his theoretical remarks reveal a view of the nature and function of poetic imagery which is both limited and naive, even when glorified with terms like *phanopoeia*. *Phanopoeia* is defined in *How to Read* as "a casting of images upon the visual imagination," a process in which, Pound adds, "we find the greatest drive toward utter precision of words." Both parts of this definition are inadequate: the first (as F. R. Leavis pointed out long ago) because it restricts the range of imagery to a single sense, and postulates a visualizing process in the poetic experience which may not, in fact, be there; the second because, while imagery may be precise, it may also be elusive, ambiguous, and indirect, and these may all be excellent qualities in a poem. Pound's concern with the concreteness of things seems to have led him to exaggerate the pictorial dimension of imagery, making a poem a kind of stereopticon performance, and neglecting other, less overtly visual qualities.

We find the same motive behind the sleight-of-hand by which Pound applies the term *ideogram* to English poetic practice. In Chinese orthography (if Fenollosa is right) it is possible to speak with some accuracy of the "presentation" of images, since the symbol for *horse,* for example, has four visible legs. But the assertion that the symbols of the English alphabet, however arranged, can do the same thing is obviously false, and *ideogrammatic* is at best a remotely figurative way of talking about poetry in English. One can see, though, how it might be a necessary figure in Pound's theory. For if you accept the principle that meaning resides in things, then you are forced to the following principle that that poem means most which is the most precise presentation of things, and the closer imagery can be brought to actual representation, the better.

The rules for writing such poetry will go something like this:

1. Direct treatment of the "thing" whether subjective or objective.
2. To use absolutely no word that does not contribute to the presentation.

These are, of course, the ground rules for Imagism, as laid down by Pound, H. D., and Richard Aldington in 1912. But they describe equally well the method of *The Cantos,* for Pound's briefest lyrics and his vast epic have a common root in the theories of the prose tradition—they all belong to one class of poetry, the poetry of things.

II

Let us consider what a thoroughgoing adherence to the prose tradition might be expected to produce in verse. One might look, first of all, for what Josephine Miles calls "phrasal poetry," a poetry, that is, in which substantives and their modifiers outnumber verbs and verbals. And indeed this does seem to be the case with Pound. In two well-known Cantos, for example—the fourteenth (the first of the Hell Cantos) and the forty-fifth ("With *Usura*")—though the Cantos differ in mood, the effect is the same in that both are essentially catalogues, Canto xiv a series of incomplete sentences without main verbs, Canto xlv a series of parallel examples. Each in its way is extremely forceful, but the force comes from the weight of the substantives and not from the pressure of verbal action. And if we look at Pound's most anthologized Imagist poem, "In a Station of the Metro," we will find that it goes right off Miss Miles's scale: she describes her poetic types in terms of the relation of the number of nouns and adjectives to the number of verbs, but "In a Station of the Metro" has no verbs at all.

It seems rather odd that a student of Fenollosa should be so indifferent to the power of verbs, for the main point of Fenollosa's theory, as described in "The Chinese Written Char-

acter as a Medium for Poetry," is that the essence of poetry is
in its verbal action, in its power to represent "things in motion."
Pound picked up the representation of things, but he seems to
have overlooked the motion. Perhaps such an oversight is to be
expected in a poetry of things.

We might also expect, though it is certainly not necessary,
that a poetry of things should minimize, or even abandon, syntactical forms. Syntax demands some nonsubstantive, and therefore insubstantial, language, and it imposes a form upon experience which is not *in* experience. In *The Cantos,* Pound has employed three kinds of syntax-substitutes: the catalogue (as in
Cantos xiv and xlv mentioned above), the associative juxtaposition, and the pattern of recurrences. These three verbal constructions come as close as one can come in words to the representation
of physical relationships—either one-after-the-other, or side-by-
side, or again-and-again. Like Hamlet to his mother, Pound tells
us to "look here upon this picture and on this"; but unlike Hamlet,
he expects that the relationship will do the job alone.

This structural mannerism has become more pronounced in
the later *Cantos.* The argument for the defense is that by now
the readers who are left are used to the method, and can recognize
allusions to earlier matter; but though this may justify increasing
condensation, it does not affect the essential problem of establishing conceptual and progressive relationships within the limitations of a purely substantive ordering.

Juxtaposed images have some of the properties of metaphor,
but they do not compose metaphors, and Pound has generally
been wary of endorsing actual metaphorical constructions. "Art
deals with certitude," he once wrote. "There is no 'certitude'

about a thing which is pretending to be another thing." And he advised young poets: "Don't mess up the perception of one sense by trying to define it in terms of another." Thus in his theorizing he emphasizes the emotional power of the thing in itself, the "natural object," and condemns ornamental metaphor as "arraying the ox with trappings"; and his enthusiasms are for writers like Joyce (the Joyce of *Dubliners* and the *Portrait*), in whom he found "a hardness and gauntness, 'like the side of an engine'; efficient; clear statement, no shadow of comment, and behind it a sense of beauty that never relapses into ornament." (Pound put Joyce with Hueffer, diametrically opposite to "the softness and mushiness of the neo-symbolist movement.")

In his principal remarks on imagery—the "Retrospect" notes, "How to Read," and "As for Imagisme"—Pound has much to say about economy and precision in presenting the image, but nothing to say about the figurative use of language. He does, to be sure, quote Aristotle on the apt use of metaphor in his "Note on Dante," but the remarks that follow make only elementary distinctions among varieties of epithets, and do not take us very far toward understanding why Aristotle should think that "the apt use of metaphor . . . is the hall-mark of genius."

Pound's mistrust of metaphor has, of course, an historical dimension: he was reacting against the conventional figures of speech—the "dim lands of peace" and "dove gray hills" of his nineteenth-century predecessors—and against what he called "the abominable dog-biscuit of Milton's rhetoric." This line of attack was necessary, and Pound deserves all honor for the beneficial operation that he performed on poetic style. But there is also, I think, an ontological point here. If reality inheres in a thing in flux, and the best poem is the "direct treatment of the thing," then figurative language is bad because it is an abstraction from reality, an imposition of intellectualized order upon the actual flux, which only offers us object beside object, event after event.

But it is impossible that a poet should altogether avoid metaphor, and Pound has ignored his own advice again and again in his best verse. In *Mauberley,* for example,

> There died a myriad,
> And of the best, among them,
> For an old bitch gone in the teeth,
> For a botched civilization.

> Charm, smiling at the good mouth,
> Quick eyes gone under earth's lid.

> For two gross of broken statues,
> For a few thousand battered books.

Here the "old bitch" and "earth's lid" are metaphorical, but one can see how Pound's mistrust of ornament has led him to use brief rather than developed figures, and to wind up the passage with nonmetaphorical substantives.

In *The Cantos,* Pound's determination to imitate the flux of experience carried him further toward pure juxtaposition of things, though the necessities of scale and theme required that he expand his notion of what a poetic "thing" was. *The Cantos,* like the little imagist poems, are commonly constructed on the building-block principle—this substantive mass is set on top of that one, and so on until a substantial unit has been built. Sometimes this is done in a simple, imagist way, with a series of pictorial images. Elsewhere the building blocks are made of less directly imagistic materials—of quotations, anecdotes, bits of history, personal reminiscences, scraps of conversation. It should be clear, however, that these all have the same relation to reality that the simple visual images have—they are all particular and substantive, manifest and not abstract. And like the elements of an imagist poem, they are related to each other, not by the artificial links of logic or of syntax or of metaphor, but simply by contiguity.

Metaphor and syntax are not the only traditional poetic resources that a thoroughgoing prose-tradition poet might be expected to suppress. "Go in fear of abstractions," Pound advised would-be poets, and he has on the whole practiced his own preaching; in *Personae* the abstractions are as rare as the rhymes. But *The Cantos* would seem to raise serious problems; one can hardly expect that a long poem concerned with Justice, Good Government, Law, Equity, and Order could get along altogether without abstract terms. And of course it doesn't. But such abstractions as do turn up in *The Cantos* are particularized, either by putting them in the mouth of a persona (as when Kung "gave the words 'order' and 'brotherly deference' ") or by representing them visually in Chinese ideograms (as, for example, "metamorphosis" in Canto lvii). Even Usury, Pound's most obsessive abstraction, is given an historical particularity by calling it *usura*. Abstractions are bird's-eye views of experience, and Pound's view is sea-level—the periplum, the level of *things*. As for the vaster human speculations,

> Of heaven, earth and of things without shadows
> Cut the cackle and do not believe 'em.

Let us pause here to gather together the assertions I have made about the nature of the prose tradition as Pound has practiced it. The hypothesis on which the whole theory rests is a simple one, a kind of naive phenomenalism. Reality consists in perceived things. Poetry is the representation of reality, and therefore concerns itself with the presentation of things, and avoids any subject which cannot be embodied in an expressed image (Kung, one recalls, "said nothing of 'the life after death' "). Starting from this view of the nature of reality, Pound has created a poetry of things, a poetry, that is, which is essentially (1) particular, not abstract; (2) substantive, rather than verbal; (3) nonmetaphorical; (4) nonsyntactical.

The problems which such a poetic method raises should be obvious enough, particularly when applied to a "poem of some length." They can be divided into two general categories: problems of poetic action and problems of poetic authority.

It seems to be axiomatic that a poem of any length must be the embodiment of change, the record of a significant process. "Life," says Aristotle, "consists in action, and its end is a mode of action, not a quality." Literature gives form to modes of action; literary form is therefore always a *from-to* form—that is, it is a model of a process of significant change. Hence Aristotle wisely concluded that action is the primary constituent of tragedy, and I think we may add of epic and other major forms as well.

Now as far as I can see, there is no action in *The Cantos*. The various juxtapositional patterns are there—scene is set against scene, person against person, the transitory against the eternal, the present against the past—and usually one can conclude that some sort of tension exists between the terms. But what one cannot conclude is that the poem advances, out of tensions to resolutions. Literally nothing happens in the poem; there are allusions, to be sure, to other works in which things happen (e.g., the Homeric business in the first Canto, and the Ovid in the second) but these allusions take their place as *things,* as artifacts in the total pattern. And though there are changes of subject—frequent and often baffling changes—the agency of change, and the direction of change, are not evident, so that the poem cannot be said to realize a "mode of action."

Both the *Odyssey* and the *Divine Comedy* are invoked in *The Cantos,* but it doesn't seem to me that there is any fundamental similarity between Pound's epic and either of the others. The latter are built upon one of the most basic models of significant change—the Symbolic Journey, from initial problem, through discovery, to resolution, from departure to arrival. *The Cantos,* however, neither departs nor arrives; it begins with a conjunction in the eleventh book of the *Odyssey,* and 109 cantos later shows no sign of ending. Nor is there any discernible voyager to do the discovering. The poem *cannot* embody action, since there is no continuing figure to be acted upon, and no temporal frame in which action might occur; this is surely a crippling, if not a fatal, limitation in an epic. It is significant, I think, that the title of the poem does not identify either its theme or its action; it is neither a Divine Comedy nor an Odyssey, and indeed one is not sure whether the title *The Cantos* should be treated as a singular collective noun or as a simple plural.

By poetic authority I mean two things. A poem has authority if one, on reading it, is conscious of direction in interpretation offered by the poem itself. This may derive from the authority of an ordered system of symbolism, whether traditional or coined; or it may derive from the authority of a clear and definite point of view, an authoritative speaking voice (what Henry James calls "the primary author"). *Leaves of Grass,* for example, draws its authority from the consistent voice of its speaker; it is, as Whitman said of it in the famous "Backward Glance" passage, "an attempt, from first to last, to put *a Person,* a human being (myself, in the latter half of the Nineteenth Century, in America,) freely, fully and truly on record." *The Waste Land,* on the other hand, depends on the ordering force of symbolism alone—in spite of Eliot's footnote on Tiresias, the poem cannot be read as the utterance of a single, embracing consciousness.

The prose tradition raises an initial difficulty in that an ordered symbolism does not seem possible in terms of things which remain things. The papers of Sigismundo Malatesta, the records of John Adams's administration, details of life in the Pisan prison camp—all these are potentially the materials of symbolism, but they cannot become fully symbolic while they remain discrete. They do, of course, incline toward symbolism, as any emotionally weighted elements in a discourse tend to, but the form in which they exist prevents their entering into a significant order.

Two of Pound's critics provide a useful example of the difficulties involved in interpreting an unordered symbolism, in their discussions of Canto xvii. This canto has three principal sections: first, a lyric passage of goddesses, landscape, and sea; then a passage describing Venice; and finally a recapitulation of the two. This is the Venice passage:

A boat came,

One man holding her sail,

Guiding her with oar caught over gunwale, saying:

"   There, in the forest of marble,

"   the stone trees—out of water—

"   the arbours of stone—

"   marble leaf, over leaf,

"   silver, steel over steel,

"   silver beaks rising and crossing,

"   prow set against prow,

"   stone, ply over ply,

"   the gilt beams flare of an evening"

Borso, Carmagnola, the men of craft, *i vitrei,*

Thither, at one time, time after time,

And the waters richer than glass,

Bronze gold, the blaze over the silver,

Dye-pots in the torch-light,

The flash of wave under prows,

And the silver beaks rising and crossing,

                Stone trees, white and rose-white in the darkness.

                "In the gloom the gold

Gathers the light about it" . . .

Of this passage, Mr. Clark Emery remarks: "That Pound recognized the Republic's earlier glory is made evident in Canto XVII, where, ascending from hell and purgatory under the guidance of Plotinus, Pound comes to an earthly paradise described in terms of Venice's architectural remains." Mr. Hugh Kenner, while conceding the beauty of the lines, finds in them an image of "a perversion of nature" which he relates to usury, and concludes that "they apotheosize the arrest of living processes." Obviously they cannot both be right; if the passage describes an earthly paradise, then it cannot be a perversion of nature. But I can find no necessary reason in the poem for choosing one reading rather than the other. The lines are beautiful; the sound of the passage demonstrates, as so much of *The Cantos* does, that Pound has a marvelous ear, and the images are richly and vividly sensuous. But in the gloom of the poem they have not gathered sufficient light about them; they do not enter a significant order.

But if the poem does not have the authority of an ordered symbolism, it might still have the authority of a single speaking voice. In modern writing this second kind of authority has tended to become prominent as the more conventional mode of ordering has been abandoned: hence, I think, the development of subjective forms like the stream-of-consciousness technique, in which mind does the ordering work, and may in fact compose the only order in an otherwise chaotic reality. Pound tells us in the *Pisan Cantos* that "the drama is wholly subjective," and in that group, at least, one is aware of an experiencing personality (as one is also in the Hell Cantos). But *The Cantos* as a whole does not assume a single, continuous speaker, or if there is one the continuity of the things he utters is not such as to define either his personality or his role in the poem. There is an "I," for example, in Canto XII, who met someone called Baldy at 24 East 47th Street, but what reason have we for assuming that this is the same person as the "I" who came to Venice in his early youth in Canto XXVI, or the "I" in Canto XLVIII who thinks that Viennese coffeehouses were established in 1600? None, so far as I can see. And there are large sections of the poem—notably the China Cantos—from which even this uncertain voice is missing.

If we refer back to Pound's definition of the prose tradition, we can see that the elimination of personality from the poem logically follows from his propositions: "It presents. It does not comment. It is irrefutable because it does not present a personal predilection for any particular fraction of the truth." It is, as I have been saying, essentially phenomenal, and since it is characteristic of phenomena that they are discontinuous, the poem is discontinuous, too. But while experience may present itself to us as a series of discontinuous phenomena, a re-creation of such a series does not in itself define the experiencing personality—for definition, we require an impression of ordering. This we do not have; the form of *The Cantos* does not define its speaker.

To my mind, then, *The Cantos* is a poem lacking in significant action, lacking in order, and lacking in authority; and all these failings derive from the theories of language, of knowledge, and of reality upon which the poem is built. It is a success insofar as it demonstrates the far extremities of a poetic method; it is a failure in that the method is inadequate to a discourse on such a scale. But in any case it is an important poem, and the prose tradition of which it is certainly the most expansive monument is something which we, as critics, must deal with. In recent criticism there has been a tendency to deplore the twentieth-century poetic revolution as an unfortunate departure from the main road of poetry, an aberration of a few perverse poets, which would better not have happened. Such pinings strike me as both idle and unhistorical. Literary history, like any other kind of history, is causally determined and nonreversible; it is the product of a complex of many forces, and not of individual poetic perversities (poets are not Paris dress-designers, whimsically raising and lowering the poetic hemline to change the fashion). *The Cantos* is there, and it is the responsibility of the critics to try to understand what it means (both in itself and as a literary symptom) and how it got there.

The question of how it got there brings us back to Walt Whitman, for the prose tradition in America seems to connect him directly with Pound. Certainly Pound accepted the idea of a radical opposition in American poetry between Whitman, the "start in the right direction," and Poe, "an exotic introduced via Mallarmé and Arthur Symons," and in this opposition he placed himself firmly on the side of Whitman. Whitman is, in fact, the only American poet with whom Pound has acknowledged any kinship, and though he has been critical and even contemptuous of Whitman's verse, he nevertheless has repeatedly asserted that Whitman is "the best America has produced." In an early essay titled "What I Feel About Walt Whitman," Pound wrote: "I honor him for he prophesied me while I can only recognize him as a forebear of whom I ought to be proud." We do not know which prophecy Pound was referring to, but no doubt he meant something like Whitman's "Poets to Come," which predicts "a new brood, native, athletic, continental, greater than before known." At any rate, Whitman was for Pound a "forebear"; "we have," he wrote, "one sap and one root."

The family resemblances are easy enough to recognize. There is the common concern with America's future, the hieratic conception of the poet, the notion that "the topmost proof of a race is its own born poetry," the inclination toward science and away from organized religion, the preoccupation with the modern, the sense of the need for new methods in new circumstances. In technique there are the catalogues, the foreign languages, the wide-ranging vocabularies, the freed meter, and a common hostility toward ornament. Whitman in his prose writings, most specifically in the 1855 Preface to *Leaves of Grass,* spells out an aesthetic which is in many respects very like Pound's. He speaks, for example, of "the beauty and sacredness of the demonstrable," and expresses a confidence in the poetic power of "real objects to-day" which resembles Pound's trust in the solid basis of things, and which leads to some of the same poetic effects—to the naming of concrete things (often in endless lists), to a relative spareness of metaphor, and to a self-determined, organic form.

One could easily extract from Whitman's writings an anthology of remarks about language which would be entirely compatible with Pound's own views: "a perfect user of words uses things"; "words become vitaliz'd, and stand for things"; "all truths lie waiting in all things"; "the substantial words are in the ground and sea." Not surprisingly, it is the substantive aspect of Whitman's verse that Pound most admired. "He does convey an image of his time," Pound wrote, "you can learn more of nineteenth-century America from Whitman than from any of the writers who either refrained from perceiving, or limited their record to what they had been taught to consider suitable literary expression." By "an image of his time" Pound pretty clearly meant a collocation of particulars, and anyone who recalls the catalogues of "Salut au Monde" and "Song of the Exposition" will recognize the appropriateness of the remark. This is the prose-tradition side of Whitman, and it is the side that has its place in the genealogy of Pound's method.

But Whitman is a good deal more than a prose-tradition poet;

the multitudes that he contains include the *other* tradition, too. *Leaves of Grass* has its place among those poems which are acts of the mind, in which words are not the names of things but the complex, magical symbols of emotions and concepts. His sense of the force of words as words is everywhere apparent in his poems: in the weight he gives to consecrated abstractions like *kosmos, Democracy, En-Masse,* and in the evident pleasure he takes in such oddities as *eidolon, Camerado, hymenee, yawp.* There is no equivalent in *The Cantos* to this sacramental use of language; Pound's diction is various enough, but it varies according to *personae*—the occasion, the *thing* dictates, and the words follow. The Whitman for whom words were magical and creative was the transcendental Whitman, the poet who dabbled in "Germanic systems" and made evolution teleological, and one would naturally expect that Pound, the poetic nominalist, would be hostile to such "cackle." The worst manifestations of this side of Whitman's verse—the vague abstractions, the imprecisions, the inspirational-oratorical periods—are quite antithetical to the prose tradition, technically as well as philosophically.

It is not surprising, then, that though the kinship was there, and Pound acknowledged it, the relationship was not an easy one. Pound never actually renounced his "pig-headed father," but he did stop mentioning him in public. The "pact" that he made in 1913 seems to have lapsed by the time Pound started on *The Cantos,* and I suspect that it was at Pound's instigation that Eliot, in 1917, insisted that "Whitman is not an influence; there is not a trace of him anywhere; Whitman and Mr. Pound are antipodean to each other."

The grounds for the alienation, in Pound's terms, are in "The Pact" itself:

> I make a pact with you, Walt Whitman—
> I have detested you long enough.
> I come to you as a grown child
> Who has had a pig-headed father;
> I am old enough now to make friends.
> It was you that broke the new wood,
> Now is a time for carving.
> We have one sap and one root—
> Let there be commerce between us.

The "new wood," I take it, is the prose tradition—the conception of a poetry of "real objects to-day." But, as Pound saw it, Whitman *broke* the new wood—a verb which suggests a rather crude approach to one's material. Pound is to be, not a breaker, but a carver; the prose tradition must be made art. For the art, he turned to other ancestors—to Flaubert and Gautier, and perhaps to a godfather called Hueffer. For Whitman, Pound came to feel, had not gone far enough:

> If you insist [he wrote] on dissecting his language you will probably find that it is wrong NOT because he broke all of what were considered in his day "the rules," but because he is spasmodically conforming to this, that, or the other; sporadically dragging in a bit of "regular" metre, using a bit of literary language, and putting his adjectives where, in the spoken tongue, they are not. His real writing occurs when he gets free of all this barbed wire.

By the time Pound began on *The Cantos* he must have felt that he had gotten free of the barbed wire himself; and so the commerce ended.

The commerce ended, but the prose tradition didn't; obviously it has had a vital, continuing existence—in *The Cantos* as well as elsewhere. Insofar as it still seems reasonable to talk of poetry as "the world which is made of whole and indefeasible objects"; insofar as we acknowledge the poetic force of things realized in their unique particularity; insofar as we look, in our poetry, for the demonstrable, and allow that it may have beauty and sacredness in itself—so far this side of Whitman may be said to be persistent.

But we must add that though he is persistent, he has not prevailed. And a good thing, too. There remains, as a counterforce, the other major modern tradition (in which, as I have said, Whitman also has his honorable place); if we have a Pound, we also have an Eliot; we have William Carlos Williams, but we also have Wallace Stevens. If we have a poetry of the demonstrable, we have also a poetry of "the imagination pressing back against the pressure of reality." Pound has taken the prose tradition about as far as it will go; but perhaps, in the end, the greatest poetry will not come from one tradition or the other, neither from pure imagination nor from the reality of things, but from an interaction between them—"the interdependence of the imagination and reality as equals."

James E. Miller, Jr.

WHITMAN AND THOMAS:

THE YAWP AND THE GAB

To find a beginning and origin for an essay at linking a nine-teenth-century American's barbaric yawp with a twentieth-century Welshman's gift of gab, we might find it profitable to go back to the impressions of a poet-critic who had no hesitation in leaping oceans and centuries to connect isolated poet-prophets by the invisible but durable bonds of their kindred imaginations. He said of two visionaries: "Their poetry has at once the melody and the laxity of a fitful stormwind; . . . being oceanic, it is troubled with violent groundswells and sudden perils of ebb and reflux, of shoal and reef, perplexing to the swimmer or the sailor; in a word . . . it partakes the powers and the faults of elemental and eternal things; . . . it is at times noisy and barren and loose, root-less and fruitless and informal; and is in the main fruitful and delightful and noble, a necessary part of the divine mechanism of things." The words are those of Algernon Swinburne and they were spoken of William Blake and Walt Whitman. I would seek to extend them to Dylan Thomas. In doing so, I shall expand upon some suggestions set forth in *Start with the Sun,* a recent book representing some of my own ideas in collaboration with the insights of my colleagues, Bernice Slote and Karl Shapiro.

I: FAINT CLEWS AND INDIRECTIONS

As Swinburne well knew, Whitman had not, before he wrote, read the works of Blake. There appears to be, however, abundant evidence that Thomas had read deeply in Whitman's *Leaves of Grass*. There is, first of all, the picture of Whitman that Thomas pinned on his study wall in Laugharne, among the monkeys and the nudes. That the picture did indeed exist, a number of witnesses have testified. The British critic Derek Stanford (who made the offhand remark in his *Dylan Thomas* that Whitman was one of Thomas's favorites) first assured me in correspondence that it did; and then John Malcolm Brinnin wrote in his *Dylan Thomas in America* about seeing it on one of his visits to Laugharne. In a 1957 radio broadcast reprinted in the 1960 *Casebook on Dylan Thomas,* Bill Read reported his "Visit to Laugharne" and Thomas's study: "Over the work-table in the shack was a large, striking photograph of Walt Whitman and under this was a smaller picture of William Blake." Swinburne would, I think, have appreciated the symbolism of the Welsh bard's daily confrontation of the wild eyes of the English mystic and the bold eyes of the American vagabond.

In trying to find some record of Thomas's feeling about Whitman, I noted Alfred Kazin's referring in his 1957 *Atlantic Monthly* article ("The Posthumous Life of Dylan Thomas") to Thomas's "beloved Whitman." In answer to my query, Kazin confessed that he was speaking entirely from memory of personal conversations with the Welsh poet: Thomas frequently held forth at length in praise of Whitman. Other friends and acquaintances of

Thomas—among them John Davenport and Vernon Watkins—
have supplied additional personal testimony as to Thomas's en-
thusiasm for Whitman.

Thomas's poem "The Countryman's Return," which had not
been brought into the *Collected Poems,* was published in Vernon
Watkins's volume of *Letters* in 1957. In Thomas's 1940 letter is
direct reference to Whitman. The surprising thing about this
comic poem is not that there is mention of Whitman in it but
that the entire poem turns out to be a satire in which Thomas
makes fun of himself as a Whitman scaled down to size. In his
letter to Watkins, Thomas called the poem a "half comic attack"
on himself: "You'll see the heavy hand with which I make fun
of this middle-class, beardless Walt who props humanity, in his
dirty, weeping, expansive moments, against corners and counter
and tries to slip, in grand delusions of all embracing humanitar-
ianism, everyone into himself."

The "rollicking attack" on himself as Whitman, which concludes with his "unrepentance of the charges," can leave little
doubt that Thomas's imagination had been strongly engaged by
Whitman's *Leaves.* Had he not been impressed so deeply, he
could not have parodied so well:

> Beggars, robbers, inveighlers,
> Voices from manholes and drains,
> Maternal short time pieces,
> Octopuses in doorways,
>
> . . . .
>
> All the hypnotised city's
> Insidious procession
> Hawking for money and pity
> Among the hardly possessed.

> And I in the wanting sway
> Caught among never enough
> Conjured me to resemble
> A singing Walt from the mower
> And jerrystone trim villas
> Of the upper of the lower half,
> Beardlessly wagging in Dean Street.

In view of Thomas's picture and talk of Whitman, and his comic vision of himself as a beardless Walt, we might expect Whitman's name to loom large in the speculations on Thomas's literary kinships. But in all the literature that has accumulated on Thomas, and among all the writers advanced as related or connected, Whitman's name is rarely found. In the first book to be written on Thomas, Henry Treece listed, "in order of the apparent strength of their influence," poets Gerard Manley Hopkins, Hart Crane, Swinburne, Rimbaud, and Francis Thompson, and he added prose writers James Joyce and Henry Miller. Derek Stanford, in his book, linked Thomas with Thomas Gray, an incongruous pairing that seems hard to hold in the mind, even though Stanford was judging quantity rather than quality. Elder Olson, in *The Poetry of Dylan Thomas,* asserted that Thomas "creates worlds in his own image, and remains the center of his own thought and feeling," and, for these reasons, "is not a Dante, a Chaucer, a Shakespeare, or a Browning, who stood inside the men they made; he is a Keats, a Byron, a Yeats, or an Eliot." Vernon Watkins, in his volume of *Letters,* spoke of Thomas's preferences from the vantage point of his personal relationship: "Dylan shared my admiration of Yeats whom he considered the greatest living poet; but Hardy was his favourite poet of the century. He disliked the sociological poetry of the thirties. My own themes were really closer to his; we were both religious poets."

A few critics have hinted at an affinity between the chants of Whitman and the songs of Thomas. John Malcolm Brinnin found Whitman's "vigor and breadth" in Thomas's poetry (*Casebook,* p. 201). Edith Sitwell, one of the first to recognize Thomas's genius, described Thomas's poetry by quoting Whitman's notebooks: "Even in religious fervor there is always a touch of animal heat" (*Casebook,* p. 125). Karl Shapiro searched through all of *Leaves* in futile pursuit of a Thomas line that seemed to echo Whitman (*Casebook,* p. 178). But these "few diffused faint clews and indirections" have been generally lost in the voluminous commentary on Thomas.

In spite of all the clues and signals that can be assembled to show that Whitman was an influence on Thomas, and in spite of what might yet be turned up in letters or reminiscences that will join their names, I do not wish to claim that Thomas derived from Whitman or that he learned from him or that he emulated him. And certainly I would not claim that Thomas's poetry is in any sense a carbon of Whitman's: the differences between Whitman's largeness and looseness and Thomas's compression and compactness, between Whitman's free verse and Thomas's formal patterns, between Whitman's public declamation and Thomas's private voice, are plain enough for all to see. I do claim, however, that Whitman and Thomas are brothers of the blood, that in their emotional response to experience they are closely akin, and that in their imaginative identification of themselves and in their visionary apprehension of their worlds they are re-

markably alike. To bring them together so as to see both at the
same time is to illuminate their separate visions by observing the
areas of impingement and the points of mergence. Let us glance
first at some of the approaches they make to their art; next look
at the pervading sexual, procreative, or Freudian imagery in
each; then touch on the bardic, elemental, or primitive strain in
their poetry; and finally examine the religious, mystical, or spiritual identity each gives to himself and to his universe.

II: YAWPING AND GABBING

Near the end of "Song of Myself," Whitman warned: "I too
am not a bit tamed, I too am untranslatable,/ I sound my barbaric
yawp over the roofs of the world." Thomas declared in "On No
Work of Words":

> To take to give is all, return what is hungrily given
> Puffing the pounds of manna up through the dew of heaven,
> The lovely gift of the gab bangs back on a blind shaft.

Whitman's *yawp* and Thomas's *gab* are almost belligerently un-
poetical and earthy, suggesting, as they do, the raucous and the
trivial. And these small but robust words are typical of both poets;
frequently they drag their diction in off the streets or find it in the
alley or pick it up around a gang of bus drivers or sailors. Derek
Stanford noted this "adaptation of colloquialisms to a lyrical end
and purpose" as one of Thomas's most important innovations.
But before him Whitman had defined the technique in a short
piece called "Slang in America": "Considering Language then
as some mighty potentate, into the majestic audience-hall of the
monarch ever enters a personage like one of Shakspere's clowns,

and takes position there, and plays a part even in the stateliest
ceremonies. Such is Slang, or indirection, an attempt of common
humanity to escape from bald literalism, and express itself illimitably, which in highest walks produces poets and poems." Thus
we have Whitman yawping and Thomas gabbing. Thus Whitman asks, "Who goes there? hankering, gross, mystical, nude,"
and he declares, "I find no sweeter fat than sticks to my own
bones." Thomas says, "And that's the rub, the only rub that
tickles," and describes himself "Dressed to die, the sensual strut
begun."

This comedy of language that turns up in so much of the poetry
of Whitman and Thomas is certainly not wit. Wit is cleverly intellectual and heads in the direction of elegance. This language-comedy is a comedy of crudeness, aimed not at inflation but deflation, designedly inelegant and sometimes downright vulgar. By
letting these clowns into their stately ceremonies, Whitman and
Thomas appear as unliterary; not as rustics but as shrewd and
rebellious primitives on the side of the unschooled and unlettered.
This role is one that both poets wanted to cultivate. Whitman
wrote (in the 1855 Preface): "The poems distilled from other
poems will probably pass away." Thomas wrote to Vernon Watkins (March 21, 1938) a criticism of Watkins's poems: "All the
words are lovely, but they *seem* so *chosen,* not struck out. I can
see the sensitive picking of words, but none of the strong, inevitable pulling that makes a poem an event, a happening, an
action perhaps, not a still-life or an experience put down, placed,
regulated . . . [many of the phrases] seem to me 'literary,' not
living. They seem, as indeed the whole poem seems, to come out
of the nostalgia of literature." Thomas added approvingly of one

poem, it "has a lot more vulgarity in it, breaches of the nostalgic etiquette."

In short, the language of Whitman and Thomas, their comedy and their vulgarity, identifies them with the unliterary and the primitive. But this identification is not one of fact and life but of imagination and drama. Whitman and Thomas are not primitives, but they assume the poetic masks of primitives. In his advice on Watkins's poem, Thomas was concerned not that the words *were* chosen and literary, but that they *seemed* so, and did not *seem* "struck out" and "living." Whitman emphasized this distinction in an early letter comparing some of his earlier with his later work: it was, he said, "certainly more perfect as a work of art, being adjusted in all its proportions, and its passion having the indispensable merit that though to the ordinary reader let loose with wildest abandon, the true artist can see it is yet under control." Both Whitman and Thomas wanted their poems to be *actions,* not *still-lifes,* and they frequently strove for effects of furious frenzy and wild abandon—but neither assumed that mere uncontrolled yawping and gabbing would achieve these effects. Both poets labored mightily over their poems, as the massive revisions in the nine lifetime editions of *Leaves of Grass* reveal for Whitman, and as the recurrent concern for word and phrase in his letters reveals for Thomas.

In their conceptions of where poems come from and how they grow Whitman and Thomas were also closely akin. Both poets were no doubt influenced by the psychology of their day, Whitman by phrenology, Thomas by Freud. More important than any question of the validity of these psychologies is the question of what imaginative use the poets made of them. If these psychologies had not existed, probably the poets would have invented their own, for they instinctively understood the deep and complex sources of their poetry in the soul-stuff of the mind. At the conclusion of a list of the phrenological attributes of the poet, Whitman says, "With a perfect sense of the oneness of nature and the propriety of the same spirit applied to human affairs . . . these [characteristics] are called up of the float of the brain of the world to be parts of the greatest poet from his birth out of his mother's womb and from her birth out of her mother's." This "float of the brain of the world," curiously close to Jung's collective unconscious, is thus the source of a poet's profoundest, most universal qualities. Thomas similarly posited some such source in the unconscious—he called it "darkness"—for the poet's subject: "Poetry is the rhythmic movement from an overclothed blindness to a naked vision. My poetry is the record of my individual struggle from darkness towards some measure of light."

Thomas, like Whitman, frequently outlined his poetics in his poems. In the "Author's Prologue" which he set at the beginning of his *Collected Poems,* he defined (like Whitman in "Inscriptions") the nature of his poems and their subject—

> as I hack
> This rumpus of shapes
> For you to know
> How I, a spinning man,
> Glory also this star, bird
> Roared, sea born, man torn, blood blest.

Man gloriously involved on this earth: for this theme a "rumpus of shapes" is indeed required. "In My Craft or Sullen Art" reveals that Thomas's poems are not for the "proud man" or the dead, "But for the lovers, their arms/ Round the griefs of the ages"; in "On No Work of Words," Thomas chides himself for not writing "for three lean months in the bloody/ Belly of the rich year," and he cries out "To take to give is all." These attitudes, these stances, this glory and anguish are familiar to the close reader of *Leaves of Grass*. Whitman exclaimed, "I . . . Know my omnivorous lines and must not write any less." Thomas, in one of the best of his poems on poetry, "Especially When the October Wind," seems devoured by his omnivorous lines as he walks along the seashore and observes a world translate itself into syllables and words. His exclamation, "By the sea's side hear the dark-vowelled birds," recalls Whitman's "Out of the Cradle Endlessly Rocking," in which a little boy, the outsetting bard, listens intently to a dark-vowelled bird and a word out of the sea. As Thomas walks in his world of nature become words, he envisions the poems he will make:

> Some let me make you of the meadow's signs;
> The signal grass that tells me all I know
> Breaks with the wormy winter through the eye.

The signal grass that tells me all I know. Whitman could well assert that the signal spear of summer grass he observed at the opening of "Song of Myself" told him all he knew, more than he dreamed: as the "uncut hair of graves," his grass too had broken with the "wormy winter through the eye."

III: SEXUAL FORCE

In a casual aside in his *Education,* Henry Adams defined a central theme in Whitman's poetry—and one that connects with Thomas: "Adams began to ponder, asking himself whether he knew of any American artist who had ever insisted on the power of sex, as every classic had always done; but he could think only of Walt Whitman. . . . All the rest had used sex for sentiment, never for force." Readers who picked up Thomas's *18 Poems* in 1934 must have felt not unlike the first readers of the 1855 edition of *Leaves of Grass.* The imagery and the themes of both books were of such unusual sexual frankness as to puzzle and to shock. Some readers were angered; others hailed brilliant, original talents. As both poets later published new volumes of poems, the concentrated procreative material became dispersed and integrated with other themes, but it was never diluted, never denied or disowned. Thomas left his original *18 Poems* standing at the opening of his *Collected Poems;* Whitman in his revisions did not measurably modify his 1855 themes.

For both poets, the emphasis on sex was not accidental but programmatic. Whitman wrote near the end of his career, "Difficult as it will be, it has become, in my opinion, imperative to achieve a shifted attitude from superior men and women towards the thought and fact of sexuality, as an element in character, personality, the emotions, and a theme in literature." In a similar vein, Thomas asserted: "Poetry, recording the stripping of the individual darkness, must, inevitably, cast light upon what has been hidden for too long, and, by so doing, make clean the naked exposure. . . . It must drag further into the clean nakedness of light more even of the hidden causes than Freud could realize." Whitman seems to speak for both poets in "Song of Myself":

> Through me forbidden voices,
> Voices of sexes and lusts, voices veil'd and I remove the veil,
> Voices indecent by me clarified and transfigur'd.

As Whitman removes the veil and Thomas strips the darkness, the hidden worlds they reveal are astonishingly similar. It is not the world of conventional love poetry but a world of sexual involvement, full of ambiguity, contrary impulses, masculine and feminine signs and symbols—the entire universe shot through with pulsing gender. In neither poet is there an attitude of extremes—shrinking horror or sentimental approbation. Rather the attitude in both is one of personal and cosmic involvement, a celebration of what *is*—with all its connotations of agony and ecstasy, pain and pleasure, life and death—as man's glorious fate and destiny. Whitman set aside, in the 1860 edition of *Leaves of Grass,* one entire section—"Children of Adam"—in which to sing the "song of procreation"; in the last poem in Thomas's *Collected Poems,* "In the White Giant's Thigh," in a kind of sexual "Elegy in a Country Churchyard," Thomas celebrated the wild, orgiastic dreams of the dead women who even in their graves "lie longing still."

Both Whitman and Thomas have been charged with obscurity and perversity. Perhaps it is inevitable that poets who would remove veils and strip darkness must deal primarily in indirection—direct assaults in scientific or clinical descriptions would surely miss the essence of sexual feeling and experience. When Whitman said, "The words of my book nothing, the drift of it everything," he seemed to speak for himself and for Thomas in their oblique approach and their symbolic techniques. And too, the poet who sets out to dramatize honestly the range and complexity of sexual feeling will render himself vulnerable, especially to the personal purist and the public moralist.

Readers of Whitman and Thomas recognize from the begin-

ning much imagery that is not only heterosexual but vaguely
onanistic and auto- and homoerotic. It is as though these poets
said—well, here is the beginning of things and here is where we
must, in all frankness, begin. Psychologists have long maintained
that the successive stages of sexual consciousness are not far
removed from those dramatized in Whitman and Thomas. In
the vivid passage on "touch" in "Song of Myself," Whitman exclaims:

> On all sides prurient provokers stiffening my limbs,
> Straining the udder of my heart for its withheld drip,
> Behaving licentious toward me, taking no denial,
> Depriving me of my best as for a purpose,
> Unbuttoning my clothes, holding me by the bare waist.

In "My Hero Bares His Nerves," Thomas writes:

> My hero bares my side and sees his heart
> Tread, like a naked Venus,
> The beach of flesh, and wind her bloodred plait;
> Stripping my loin of promise,
> He promises a secret heat.

These ambiguous passages, so close in both imagery and sensibility, portray the poets emotionally paralyzed by a force beyond
their power. The feelings defined do not radiate *out* but *in,* to the
exposed and naked self. These emotions are not the emotions of
love, nor were meant to be; they are the crude raw lump of feeling out of which love might be refined.

But there are many passages, too, that are filled with sexual
symbolism whose dense and compacted meaning is unraveled only
at great expense of intellectual energy—and even then with un-

certainty. The following two stanzas might have been written by either or both of the poets:

First:

> The cloth laps a first sweet eating and drinking,
> Laps life-swelling yolks . . . . laps ear of rose-corn, milky
>   and just ripened:
> The white teeth stay, and the boss-tooth advances in darkness,
> And liquor is spilled on lips and bosoms by touching glasses,
>   and the best liquor afterward.
>
>   ("The Sleepers," 1855 version, ll. 67–70)

And second:

> When once the twilight locks no longer
> Locked in the long worm of my finger
> Nor damned the sea that sped about my fist,
> The mouth of time sucked, like a sponge,
> The milky acid on each hinge,
> And swallowed dry the waters of the breast.
>
>   ("When Once the Twilight Locks No Longer")

Of course the technique here reveals the poet, the long flowing line betraying Whitman, the formality informing on Thomas. But if we were left to judge by the imagery alone, I think that we might not know so easily that the first is Whitman's and the second Thomas's. In both instances, I believe, we have passages which are essentially unparaphrasable: the images have grown and bred into exotic and enigmatic clusters to mean nothing but themselves and to make whatever primal appeal they can make to the lower levels of consciousness, where rational and irrational meet and entangle.

In portraying sex as force, both Whitman and Thomas extend
the sexual drama to the cosmos, identifying man's procreative
energies with the primeval forces that motivate all nature. Both
poets could imagine vividly their prenatal life in evolutionary and
biological terms that ranged far beyond mere personal involvement. Whitman looks back at himself in the depths of time:

> Before I was born out of my mother generations guided me,
> My embryo has never been torpid, nothing could overlay it.
>
> For it the nebula cohered to an orb,
> The long slow strata piled to rest it on,
> Vast vegetables gave it sustenance,
> Monstrous sauroids transported it in their mouths and de-
> posited it with care.
>
> ("Song of Myself," 1881 version, Section 44)

Thomas dramatically reconstructs the event of his own conception:

> I dreamed my genesis in sweat of sleep, breaking
> Through the rotating shell, strong
> As motor muscle on the drill, driving
> Through vision and the girdered nerve.
>
> ("I Dreamed My Genesis")

Clearly both poets envision compelling natural forces, dynamically
sexual and generative, that work in cosmic harmony with the
procreative rhythms of man.

This projection of the sexual vision to the world and the universe is not always translated into personal terms. Frequently
the whole of nature itself is pictured as pulsing with sexual feeling. Whitman paints a landscape:

Hefts of the moving world at innocent gambols silently
    rising, freshly exuding,
Scooting obliquely high and low.

Something I cannot see puts upward libidinous prongs,
Seas of bright juice suffuse heaven.

("Song of Myself," Section 24)

Thomas walks along the sea:

And yellow was the multiplying sand,
Each golden grain spat life into its fellow,
Green was the singing house.

("From Love's First Fever to Her Plague")

For both Whitman and Thomas, the sexual drama touches on
the inmost secrets of life itself. In procreation man participates
in the pageantry of the endlessly re-created universe itself. In
his sex lies the mystery of his identification with the most vital
and ancient sources of the world's energy:

Urge and urge and urge,
Always the procreant urge of the world.

("Song of Myself," Section 3)

IV: BARDIC TONE

Of all modern poets, Thomas seems one of the few worthy of
sharing with Whitman the title of bard, with all its connotations
of seer, prophet, soothsayer, truth-giver, keeper and dispenser of
the race's wisdom, chanter of verses flowing with visions, singer
of songs that tally with the soul. Both poets opened their books
announcing their roles as singers. "One's-self I sing, a simple

separate person," said Whitman—"The Modern Man I sing."
Thomas began:

> At poor peace I sing
> To you strangers (though song
> Is a burning and crested act,
> The fire of birds in
> The world's turning wood,
> For my sawn, splay sounds),
> Out of these seathumbed leaves
> That will fly and fall
> Like leaves of trees. . .

Whitman's *Leaves of Grass,* like Thomas's seathumbed "leaves
of trees," is "ocean's poem," and takes to itself the authority of
the rude, undisciplined, living, perpetuating and dying, natural
world.

When they announce themselves as singers, Whitman and
Thomas reveal that their intention is celebration, celebration of
the natural and the primitive, the elemental and the generative,
the forces and energies that drive life through its endless cycles of
mystic origin, generation, and dissolution. The conversational
tone, the world-weary, sophisticated measure, the tinkling pretti-
ness of fireside chatter, the pompous ring of moralizing clichés
—none of these will do. The bard must chant in his own voice as
his vision informs him. Though Whitman's verse is free and
Thomas's measured (and both, of course, more disciplined than
meets the eye), Whitman's rude songs share with Thomas's
"rumpus of shapes" an effect of copious abundance, frenzied
eruption, turbulent spouting and gushing. More frequently than

not their poems burst open—"Out of the cradle endlessly rocking,"
"When, like a running grave, time tracks you down"—and immediately tumble the reader in the forward sweep and flow of the
poem, involving and carrying him even against his will, not
with a logic of words but by the frantic compulsion of the heaping
images and the wild thumping of the elemental rhythms.

As bards of the natural and primitive, Whitman and Thomas
are poets of the birds and the beasts; for in the beauty and dignity
of animals, in their fierce hungers and in their unquestioning
involvement, in their physical grace and unselfconsciousness, man
can see reflected the possibilities of his own suppressed and ex-
cessively refined physical nature. In "Song of Myself," Whitman
exclaims:

> I think I could turn and live with animals, they're so placid
>   and self-contain'd,
> I stand and look at them long and long.
>
> They do not sweat and whine about their condition,
> They do not lie awake in the dark and weep for their sins.

In his Prologue poem, Thomas becomes a modern Noah as he
gathers about him in his ark singing in the sun:

> . . . animals thick as thieves
> On God's rough tumbling grounds
> (Hail to His beasthood!).
> Beasts who sleep good and thin,
> Hist, in hogsback woods!

There is abundant variety in the animal imagery in both poets,
but perhaps the most memorable is that of the birds. Whitman

gave major dramatic and symbolic roles to birds in some of his greatest poems—the mockingbirds in "Out of the Cradle," and the hermit thrush in "When Lilacs Last in the Dooryard Bloom'd." In shorter poems like "The Dalliance of Eagles," he used winged creatures to symbolize his central themes. On Thomas's ark are owls, doves, rooks, and curlews, and the birds fly in and out of all his poems. But the drama of the birds reaches a climax in "Over Sir John's Hill," with the poet turned fabling Aesop observing with the priestly heron the "hawk on fire" ravenously preying on the smaller sparrows. The poet and the heron look on silently at this almost merry struggle of life and death, and hear at the close of the poem the music of the "wear-willow river" for the "sake of the souls of the slain birds sailing." The entire mood of the poem is reminiscent in a way of the tone of Whitman's "I Sit and Look Out," in which the poet observes the drama of the world's struggle and agony—sees, hears, and is silent.

Both Whitman and Thomas, as poets of elemental nature, know that life involves dissolution, that the beginning is but prelude to the end, that birth can lead only to death, as awakening must be followed by a sleeping. If Whitman and Thomas are poets of procreation and life, they are also the poets of death. The theme of death runs through all of *Leaves of Grass,* sometimes scattered through the individual poems, sometimes concentrated in a single section, like "Whispers of Heavenly Death." All the great poems involve death on some level. In "Song of Myself" the poet exclaims, "And as to you Death, and you bitter hug of mortality, it is idle to try to alarm me." In "Out of the Cradle" "death" is the word hissed by the sea's rim to the listening boy. In "When Lilacs Last in the Dooryard Bloom'd," death becomes the "Dark mother always gliding near with soft feet." Likewise in Thomas death threads its constant way through his poetry. All the birthday poems embrace the thought of death: in "Twenty-four Years" the poet is "Dressed to die"; in "Poem in October" he celebrates his "thirtieth year to heaven"; and "Poem on His Birthday" concludes, "As I sail out to die" (reminiscent of Whitman's "Now land and life finalè and farewell" as he sails forth in "Songs of Parting"). Thomas's title for his 1946 volume, *Deaths and Entrances,* intentionally reverses the expected order of the words. He advises his father, "Do not go gentle into that good night"; "Though wise men at their end know dark is right," he reasons, every man should live his life to its fullest fire and rage. Thomas's most passionate statement of his theme is in "And Death Shall Have No Dominion."

> Though they be mad and dead as nails,
> Heads of the characters hammer through daisies.

Like Whitman envisioning the "curling grass" as transpiring from the "breasts of young men" or from "mother's laps," Thomas invokes an image of continuity in nature that deprives death of all his kingdom.

For man in his generative, procreative identity is inextricably involved in the continuous and cyclic processes of nature. He is created out of these natural processes and he returns to them, contributing to their continuing evolution. Whitman wears the evolutionary past proudly like a uniform—as a symbol of his origins and destiny:

> I find I incorporate gneiss, coal, long-threaded moss, fruits,
>   grains, esculent roots,

And am stucco'd with quadrupeds and birds all over,
And have distanced what is behind me for good reasons.

("Song of Myself," Section 31)

In his rewriting of the story of Genesis, Thomas similarly envisions the origins of human vitality as coeval with the beginning of world matter:

Before the veins were shaking in their sieve,
Blood shot and scattered to the winds of light
The ribbed original of love.

("I Dreamed My Genesis")

Like Whitman, Thomas fuses in a direct identity the evolutionary forces with the generative energies of life:

The force that through the green fuse drives the flower
Drives my green age; that blasts the roots of trees
Is my destroyer.
And I am dumb to tell the crooked rose
My youth is bent by the same wintry fever.

The same force that grants to man his individual identity also assures his ultimate dispersal; the evolutionary life-force, with its procreative urge, urge, urge, continuously creates and destroys, embracing and enfolding all—the quadruped, the man, the rose, the spear of summer grass—into its own deep ends and destiny.

V: RELIGIOUS VISION

In spite of their emphasis on physicality, on procreative energy and elemental matter, Whitman and Thomas may well claim the title of religious poet. Near the beginning of his *Leaves*, Whitman asserted:

> Know you, solely to drop in the earth the germs of a greater
>   religion,
> The following chants each for its kind I sing.

And he once described the "purpose enclosing all" of his book
as his attempt to record his "entire faith and acceptance." Thomas
wrote at the opening of his book that his poems were written
"for the love of Man and in praise of God." But though they are
both in some sense religious poets, neither Whitman nor Thomas
is a poet of religion—like T. S. Eliot, for example. Intellectual
rather than intuitive, elegant and conversational rather than rude
and bardic, the poetry of T. S. Eliot has become the archetypal
religious poetry of our time. But above all Eliot's poetry is a
poetry of tradition, even in its mysticism; the theory behind it
is the highly intellectualized theory of the objective correlative,
the ideal of an essentially nonemotional, impersonal poetry. His
poems of religion are cerebral, and tend toward the institutional
and orthodox. The poetry of Whitman and Thomas is, in almost
all respects, at the opposite pole from the poetry of Eliot. Charged
with deep emotion and highly personal, their religious poetry
appears intuitive, defiant of institutions, careless of orthodoxy.

This is not to say, however, that Whitman and Thomas never
use traditional figures and symbols of Christianity in their poetry.
Both use them, Thomas probably more than Whitman, but mostly
in heretical or ambiguous ways. In a key passage in "Song of
Myself," Whitman assumes for a time the role of Christ:

> That I could forget the mockers and insults!
> That I could forget the trickling tears and the blows of the
>   bludgeons and hammers!

That I could look with a separate look on my own crucifixion
and bloody crowning!

. . . .

Corpses rise, gashes heal, fastenings roll from me.
I troop forth replenish'd with supreme power, one of an
average unending procession.

Thomas seems to make a similar identification with Christ in
Sonnet VIII of his sonnet sequence, "Altarwise by Owl-Light":

This was the crucifixion on the mountain,
Time's nerve in vinegar, the gallow grave
As tarred with blood as the bright thorns I wept

. . . .

I by the tree of thieves, all glory's sawbones

. . .

Suffer the heaven's children through my heartbeat.

Whitman's most clearly religious poems appear in the latter
sections of *Leaves of Grass,* and include such signal works as
"Passage to India," "Prayer of Columbus," and "Chanting the
Square Deific." Among Thomas's poems, the most religious in
the traditional sense seem to be the sonnet sequence, "Altarwise by Owl-Light," "There Was a Saviour," and the visually
patterned series, "Vision and Prayer."

But it would be wrong to suggest that even in these poems
emphasizing religious themes there is a final commitment, in
either Whitman or Thomas, to the traditional Christian attitudes
found in Eliot's religious poetry—the oppressive sense of sin,
the self-revulsion and self-negation, the search for redemption
through self-mortification. There are, however, moments of

mystical merging in Whitman and Thomas. In "Passage to India," the poet cries out in his mystic vision:

> Bathe me O God in thee, mounting to thee,
> I and my soul to range in range of thee.

Thomas experiences a similar mystical mergence in "Vision and Prayer";

> But the loud sun
>   Christens down
>   The sky.
>   I
>   Am found.
>
>   . . . .
>
> Now I am lost in the blinding
> One.

But such moments of religious ecstasy, of mystical union and identification, can be seen as complementary to the essential primitivism and physical celebration of the two poets. Symbolic of their attitude of translating Christianity into their own semi-pagan terms of life-affirmation and celebration is the way in which they refer to the deity in familiar terms—bringing him down to the level of their own human-divinity. Whitman made him a brother—

> As fill'd with friendship, love complete, the Elder Brother found,
> The Younger melts in fondness in his arms.

Thomas's familiar term makes him into the man next door:

> My Jack of Christ born thorny on the tree.

But when Whitman referred to his religious themes and
Thomas said his poems were in praise of God, they were surely
not referring to those few poems in their work that can be
singled out and narrowly labeled religious. On the contrary they
were talking about currents that run strongly through all their
poetry—the spiritual vision that pervades their most procreative
and physical poems, the celebration of human involvement in
the processes of the natural world, the identification of man's
energies with the mysterious forces of the cosmic drama. For the
materials of this poetry they turned not to the divinity of religious
orthodoxy but to the divinity of their own deeply involved human nature. Whitman declared, in "Song of Myself":

> Walt Whitman, a kosmos, of Manhattan the son,
> Turbulent, fleshy, sensual, eating, drinking and breeding.

In a whole series of songs of the self—"Twenty-four Years,"
"Poem in October," "Fern Hill," "Poem on His Birthday"—
Thomas also discovered the cosmos in his own spirit and celebrated creation by celebrating himself. In his October poem, he
evoked the vital material world of his full, free boyhood, and
sang of his joy in the mystery:

> These were the woods the river and sea
>   Where a boy
> In the listening
> Summertime of the dead whispered the truth of his joy
> To the trees and the stones and the fish in the tide.
>   And the mystery
>   Sang alive
> Still in the water and singingbirds.

"Poem on His Birthday," one of Thomas's last poems, seems an attempt to sum up the meager wisdom of the poet in the experience of his thirty-five years:

> Four elements and five
> Senses, and man a spirit in love
> Tangling through this spun slime
> To his nimbus bell cool kingdom come

This is man in the full faith of his acceptance, celebrating life on its own exacting terms, heading toward the future fully involved and engaged. Whitman said:

> This then is life,
> Here is what has come to the surface after so many throes
>   and convulsions.
>
>
> How curious! how real!
> Underfoot the divine soil, overhead the sun.

Thomas imagines a universe celebrating his progress through life to the end:

> . . . the closer I move
> To death, one man through his sundered hulks,
>   The louder the sun blooms
> And the tusked, ramshackling sea exults.

Whitman's vision of his own dissolution at the end of "Song of Myself" portrays a world similarly engaged in his destiny:

> The last scud of day holds back for me,
> It flings my likeness after the rest and true as any on the
>   shadow'd wilds,
> It coaxes me to the vapor and the dusk.

Religion for Whitman and Thomas constituted not an embrace of the church but a celebration of man divinely alive in all his senses and being. To them the greatest spiritual miracles were the physical facts of birth, generation, and death. Their exultation in life did not falter at death. Their religious faith was that the final dissolution, however personally agonizing, was simply another beginning, a reinvolvement in the generative forces of the ceaselessly evolving universe.

I started at the beginning with the words of Swinburne on Whitman and Blake because I thought they pointed in the right direction. His words seem also to offer a fair summary of what I have tried to show. Of the American and British poets he said: "To each all sides and shapes of life are alike acceptable or endurable. From the fresh free ground of either workman nothing is excluded that is not exclusive. The words of either strike deep and run wide and soar high. They are both full of faith and passion, competent to love and to loathe, capable of contempt and worship." From his chair at his study desk, Thomas could look out and see the cliff's trees, the ocean's rim, the sea's waves, and the sky of birds beyond. And if his glance turned to his study walls, he could gaze into the bold eyes of Whitman, the wild eyes of Blake. Was he not heir of all he saw? Was he not blood-brother to these poets of the "elemental and eternal things"?

James A. Wright

THE DELICACY OF

WALT WHITMAN

The public mask, the coarse Whitman, is false. Then what is true? Is there a private Whitman who is delicate, and if there *is* a delicate Whitman, what is his poetry like? Where can we find it? And what does it have to do with those of us who want to read it? Is Whitman's delicacy a power that is alive in American poetry at the present moment? If so, who is displaying it? And is it capable of growth?

The *delicacy* of Walt Whitman. I do not mean to imply that Whitman was delicate as Nietzsche, for example, was in delicate health. Whitman really does seem to have been a strong man, in spite of the public mask's strident insistence on his own vigor. His actions were often modest and yet they demonstrate a physical condition astonishingly robust. When the war began, Whitman was forty-two years old. He went into the war. He did not have to go. I am not concerned with arguing the ethical significance of his relation to the war. I point only to the fact. In an essay recently published in the *Sewanee Review*, Mr. James M. Cox eloquently describes Whitman's exploit in terms which reveal the abundant physical strength of the man:

Whitman's role in the Civil War stands as one of the triumphs of our culture. That this figure should have emerged from an almost illiterate background to become a national poet, that he should have at the age of forty-two gone down into the wilderness of Virginia to walk across the bloody battlefields ministering to the sick and wounded, that he should have paced through the hospitals and kept a vigil over the mutilated victims on both sides, that he should have created the war in prose and poetry of an extraordinarily high order—that he should have done these deeds shows how truly he had cast himself in the heroic mould.

So the delicacy I have in mind is not an empty gentility, nor the physical frailty that sometimes slithers behind arrogance. It is the delicacy of his *poetry* that concerns me. It has its source in the character of Whitman himself, and it is, I believe, available to American poetry at the present time.

Whitman's poetry has delicacy of music, of diction, and of form. The word "delicacy" can do without a rhetorically formal definition; but I mean it to suggest powers of restraint, clarity, and wholeness, all of which taken together embody that deep spiritual inwardness, that fertile strength, which I take to be the most beautiful power of Whitman's poetry, and the most readily available to the poetry, and indeed the civilization, of our own moment in American history.

If what I say is true, then we are almost miraculously fortunate to have Whitman available to us. For some time the features of American poetry most in evidence have been very different from Whitman's: in short, recent American poetry has often been flaccid, obtuse and muddied, and fragmentary, crippled almost. Yet there is great talent alive in our country today, and if the spirit of Whitman can help to rescue that talent from the fate of so many things in America, that begin nobly and end meanly, then we ought to study him as carefully as we can. What is his poetry like?

Let us consider first the delicacy of his music. And since I want to listen to the music closely, a few notes on traditional prosody are in order. At this point Whitman himself is ready to help us. As a stylist, he did not begin as a solitary barbarian (in Ortega's sense of that word). He is many things that are perhaps discomforting and even awkward, but he is not a smug fool—he is not an imitation Dead End Kid pretending that no poet or man of any kind ever existed before he was born upon the earth. Whitman realizes that the past has existed.

He also understands how the past continues to exist: it exists in the present, and comes into living form only when some individual man is willing to challenge it. Whitman dares, like Nietzsche, to challenge not only what he dislikes but also what he *values.* "The power to destroy or remould," writes Whitman in the 1855 Preface to *Leaves of Grass,* "is freely used by him [the greatest poet] but never the power of attack. What is past is past. If he does not expose superior models and prove himself by every step he takes he is not what is wanted."

It seems to me of the gravest importance that Whitman's relation to established traditional forms of poetry and of society itself be clarified, so that we may free him from the tone of pretentious ignorance that has been associated with his mere name, from time to time, by fools. He knows that the past exists, and he knows that, as a poet and as a man, he has a right to live. His duty to the past is precisely this: to have the courage to live and to create his own poetry.

This is the great way of learning from the noble spirits of the past. And the most difficultly courageous way of asserting the shape and meaning of one's own poetry and one's own life is to challenge and surpass those very traditions and masters whom one can honestly respect. This deep spiritual kinship between a truly original man and the nobility of the past is formulated thus by Goethe: "People always talk of the study of the ancients; but what does that mean, except that it says, turn your attention to the real world, and try to express it, for that is what the ancients did when they were alive" (*Conversations with Eckermann*). And so in Whitman's music we find him turning away from one masterfully delicate verbal musician, Longfellow, toward the real world. Whitman respected Longfellow for his true gifts, as we ought to do. Our own scorn of Longfellow is cant. It is like the scorn of the great Victorian Englishmen that prevailed until recently under the influence of Lytton Strachey; we scurry forth like insects to deface them as soon as a serious, honorable man like Strachey assures us that Dickens, Tennyson, and Florence Nightingale are safely dead. So let us turn, for just a moment, to Longfellow, whose lovely poetry, even in his own time, was in the strict sense a musical embodiment of the European past. In *Specimen Days* ("My Tribute to Four Poets"), Whitman records a visit to Longfellow which unmistakably reveals his true respect for the poet who was almost universally celebrated as the great poet whom Whitman himself would like to be: "I shall not soon forget his lit-up face," says Whitman, "and glowing warmth and courtesy in the modes of what is called the old school." And then Whitman suddenly, and rather startlingly, remarks on his own poetic relation to Longfellow and others (Emerson, Whittier, and Bryant):

> In a late magazine one of my reviewers, who ought to know better, speaks of my "attitude of contempt and scorn and intolerance" toward the leading poets—of my "deriding" them, and preaching their "uselessness." If anybody cares to know what I think—and have long thought and avow'd—about them, I am entirely willing to propound. I can't imagine any better luck befalling these States for a poetical beginning and initiation than has come from Emerson, Longfellow, Bryant, and Whittier. . . . Longfellow for rich color, graceful forms and incidents—all that makes life beautiful and love refined—competing with the singers of Europe on their own ground, and with one exception, better and finer work than that of any of them.

Furthermore Whitman's deep humility (an intellectual as well as a moral virtue) appears in his note on the "Death of Longfellow" (*Specimen Days*). There, in the very act of praising Longfelow for his best gift ("verbal melody") he speaks of his radical inadequacy; and thus Whitman inadvertently, almost as an afterthought, identifies his own great strength:

> Longfellow in his voluminous works seems to me to be eminent in the style and forms of poetical expression that mark the present age, (an idiosyncrasy, almost a sickness, of verbal melody,). . . . He is certainly the sort of bard and counter-actant most needed for our materialistic, self-assertive,

money-worshipping, Anglo-Saxon races, and especially for
the present age in America—an age tyrannically regulated
with reference to the manufacturer, the merchant, the finan-
cier, the politician and the day workman—for whom and
among whom he comes as the poet of melody, courtesy, deference—*poet of the mellow twilight of the past* in Italy, Ger-
many, Spain, and Northern Europe. . . . He strikes a
splendid average, and does not sing exceptional passions, or
humanity's jagged escapades. He is not revolutionary, brings
nothing offensive or new, does not deal hard blows. . . . His
very anger is gentle, is at second hand, (as in the "Quadroon
Girl" and the "Witnesses.") . . . To the ungracious com-
plaint-charge of his want of racy nativity and special originality, I shall only say that America and the world may well be
reverently thankful—can never be thankful enough—for any
such singing-bird vouchsafed out of the centuries, without
asking that the notes be different from those of other song-
sters; adding what I have heard Longfellow himself say, that
ere the New World can be worthily original, and announce
herself and her own heroes, she must be well saturated with
the originality of others, and respectfully consider the heroes
that lived before Agamemnon.

The whole passage is moved by an impulse to pass beyond. Not
merely to pass beyond what one hates—the phoniness, the counter-
feit poetry which is always among us in its thousand blind, mean,
sly forms. But to pass beyond what one loves, to open one's ears,
to know what one is doing and why. It is a noble statement by
a delicate and reverent man.

Let us apply the statement to Whitman's own music. In effect, he tunes his verses toward those very crass and difficult subjects which Longfellow (for whatever reason) avoided. And yet, even so, Whitman's music is not "jagged" like the escapades of that American humanity he often sings of. It is a *delicate* music, a deeper sound than that of Longfellow; it is alive, and it hurts, as men are hurt on the jagged edges of their own lives.

So Whitman respected Longfellow, a traditional prosodist. In spite of his poems like "Evangeline," which we are told to read as though they were written in the classical dactylic hexameter, Longfellow is predominantly an iambic writer. Moreover, he writes the iambic meter with a masterful grasp of its permissive variations: the elisions, the trochaic substitutions, the spondaic effects and their euphonious combination within regular iambic patterns. But Longfellow does not write about American life. He does not write about its externals. And, shunning its externals, he does not penetrate to its spirit. Whitman notices these radical limits in the very act of praising Longfellow for his mastery— mastery of a kind which forces him to turn away from the living world and to sing either of Europe or of the American past.

Whitman also brings a rare technical understanding of prosody to bear on the living American present. But in his concern to surpass tradition, he deliberately shuns the iambic measure and all its variations, except in a very few instances (like the notorious "O Captain! My Captain!" and the less frequently quoted "Ethopia Saluting the Colors") which offer a helpful contrast to the inventive delicacy of music in Whitman's greater poems.

He shuns the iambic measure. He says, in the 1855 Preface, "The rhythm and uniformity of perfect poems show the free growth of metrical laws, and bud from them as unerringly and

loosely as lilacs and roses on a bush, and take shapes as compact
as the shapes of chestnuts and oranges." Does Whitman mean
that "free growth" is aimless? No, he speaks of "metrical laws."
Listen to his poem "Reconciliation":

> Word over all, beautiful as the sky,
> Beautiful that war and all its deeds of carnage must in time
>   be utterly lost,
> That the hands of the sisters Death and Night incessantly
>   softly wash again, and ever again, this soil'd world;
> For my enemy is dead, a man divine as myself is dead,
> I look where he lies white-faced and still in the coffin—I draw
>   near,
> Bend down and touch lightly with my lips the white face
>   in the coffin.

We cannot understand this poem's music in traditional prosodic
terms. Still, it's fun to note that Whitman did not write non-
iambic verse out of pique at his inability to control its rules. Listen
again to Whitman's opening line: "Word over all, beautiful as
the sky." The line is a flawless iambic pentameter; he uses a
trochaic substitution in the first foot, a hovering spondaic echo
between the second and third feet, a daring and yet perfectly
traditional inversion; and he successfully runs two light stresses
before the final strong stress.

It seems to me wonderful that Whitman should have written
that line, which is not only iambic, but as bold in its exploitation
of the iambic possibilities as the masters themselves: Campion,
Herrick, Wyatt, even Milton. And that is not so strange. In a note
on "British Literature" (*Collect: Notes Left Over*), Whitman

writes the following: "To avoid mistake, I would say that I not only commend the study of this literature, but wish our sources of supply and comparison vastly enlarged." The trouble is that "the British element these states hold, and have always held, enormously beyond its fit proportions . . . its products are no models for us." So he does not hate traditional British prosody, which is of course predominantly iambic. He loves its great craft, and he shows his ability to emulate it. But he is an adventurer; he wants to listen beyond the admittedly rich music of iambic, and to report what he hears.

In prosody, then, Whitman is sometimes a destroyer, but we must see that he knows exactly what he is destroying. He is both theoretically and practically ready to replace it with a new prosody of his own. He begins with a supremely sensitive ear for the music of language; he moves beyond the permissive variations of iambic; and he is not afraid of the new musical possibilities out there, so he brings some of them back with him. Perhaps they were there all the time; perhaps they are the quantitative possibilities of the classical languages that have drifted around in English. In any case, the iambic conventions do not seem to make much provision for them; and yet they can be incredibly beautiful in Whitman. We need only listen:

> Come lovely and soothing death,
> Undulate round the world, serenely arriving, arriving,
> In the day, in the night, to all, to each,
> Sooner or later delicate death.

Whitman really does have something to teach current American poets, in spite of his entering American poetry once again, in

Mr. Randall Jarrell's wicked phrase, as "the hero of a de Mille movie about Whitman"—a movie, one might add, which co-stars the Dead End Kids.

To summarize, Whitman can teach us about some possibilities of musical delicacy in our language. He sympathetically understood iambic forms (exemplified by Longfellow) which in his own poems he is trying to break and surpass. He can also teach courage, for he has great rhythmical daring; he seeks constantly for a music which really echoes and fulfills his imaginative vision.

He becomes a great artist by the ways of growth which Nietzsche magnificently describes in the first speech of *Thus Spake Zarathustra:* the Three Metamorphoses of the Spirit. The spirit that truly grows, says Nietzsche, will first be a camel, a beast of burden, who labors to bear the forms of the past, whether in morality or art or anything else; then he will change into a lion, and destroy not merely what he hates but even what he loves and understands; and the result of this concerned and accurate destruction will be the spirit's emergence as a child, who is at last able to create clearly and powerfully from within his own imagination.

Whitman says of the great poet, "He swears to his art, I will not be meddlesome, I will not have in my writings any elegance, or effect, or originality, to hang in the way between me and the rest like curtains. I will have nothing hang in the way, not the richest curtains" (Preface, 1855). And Whitman is well aware of the many curtains that can hang in the way. There is not only the old-world elegance of Longfellow—which may stand for the prosodic traditions of England, beautiful in themselves—but there is also the curtain of aimless destructiveness, which is eventually not even destructive but just trivial. In "After Trying a Certain Book" (*Specimen Days*), Whitman says that the difficulty of explaining what a poem means is not to be taken as evidence that the poem means nothing: "Common teachers or critics are always asking 'What does it mean?' Symphony of fine musician, or sunset, or sea-waves rolling up the beach—what do they mean? Undoubtedly in the most subtle-elusive sense they mean something—but who shall fathom and define those meanings? (*I do not intend this as a warrant for wildness and frantic escapades. . . .*)" (My italics.) Every scholar and every Beat who mentions Whitman ought to read that salutary note beforehand.

   Now I want to speculate on the delicacy of Whitman's diction, his choice of words. What is remarkable is not merely his attempt to include new things—objects, persons, places, and events—in his poems. Something more interesting and complex goes on: in the face of this sometimes difficult and prosaic material ("humanity's jagged escapades"), he is able to retain his delicacy, which is a power of mind as well as a quality of kindness. In a crisis, he keeps his head and his feelings alert. He can be as precise as Henry James, as Mr. Jarrell rightly says; but he is sensitively precise about things that are often in themselves harsh, even brutal.
   Mr. Jarrell has written one of the liveliest accounts of Whitman's delicacy of diction, and I refer the reader to that essay. Perhaps Mr. Jarrell does not sufficiently emphasize the enormous strength and courage it required even to face some of the horrible things Whitman faced, much less to claim them for the imagination by means of a diction that is as delicate as that of Keats.
   One of my favorite poems in Whitman is "A March in the

Ranks Hard-prest, and the Road Unknown" from *Drum-Taps*.
It reveals perfectly what I mean about Whitman's delicate diction:
his power of retaining his sensitivity right in the face of realities
that would certainly excuse coarseness, for the sake of self-defense
if for no other reason. But Whitman does not defend himself.
As he had told us in a Virgilian line, one of the noblest lines
of poetry ever written, "I was the man, I suffered, I was there."
The line is great because it is not a boast but a modest bit of
information, almost as unobtrusive as a stage-direction or perhaps
a whispered aside to the reader. (Whitman is always whispering
to us—that is another of his musical delicacies.) There he certainly
is, gathering the horror into his delicate words, soothing it if
possible, always looking at it and in the deepest sense imagining
it:

> A march in the ranks hard-prest, and the road unknown,
> A route through a heavy wood with muffled steps in the
>   darkness,
> Our army foil'd with loss severe, and the sullen remnant re-
>   treating,
> Till after midnight glimmer upon us the lights of a dim-
>   lighted building,
> We come to an open space in the woods, and halt by the
>   dim-lighted building,
> 'Tis a large old church at the crossing roads, now an im-
>   promptu hospital,
> Entering but for a minute I see a sight beyond all the pictures
>   and poems ever made,
> Shadows of deepest, deepest black, just lit by moving candles
>   and lamps,

And by one great pitchy torch stationary with wild red flame
and clouds of smoke,

By these, crowds, groups of forms vaguely I see on the floor,
some in the pews laid down,

At my feet more distinctly a soldier, a mere lad, in danger of
bleeding to death, (he is shot in the abdomen,)

I stanch the blood temporarily, (the youngster's face is white
as a lily,)

Then before I depart I sweep my eyes o'er the scene fain to
absorb it all,

Faces, varieties, postures beyond description, most in obscurity, some of them dead,

Surgeons operating, attendants holding lights, the smell of
ether, the odor of blood,

The crowd, O the crowd of the bloody forms, the yard outside
also fill'd,

Some on the bare ground, some on planks or stretchers, some
in the death-spasm sweating,

An occasional scream or cry, the doctor's shouted orders or
calls,

The glisten of the little steel instruments catching the glint of
the torches,

These I resume as I chant, I see again the forms, I smell the
odor,

Then hear outside the orders given, *Fall in, my men, fall in;*

But first I bend to the dying lad, his eyes open, a half-smile
gives he me,

Then the eyes close, calmly close, and I speed forth to the
darkness,

Resuming, marching, ever in darkness marching, on in the
ranks,
The unknown road still marching.

I want to draw attention to a single small detail of diction,
which becomes huge because of its delicacy. I mean the phrase
about the wounded young man's face. He suddenly looms up out
of the confusion and darkness; he has been shot in the abdomen;
and his face, buffaloed by shock, is "white as a lily."

There have been many poets in America who would compare
a white face with a lily. There are also many poets who attempt
to deal with a subject matter that is, like Whitman's, very far
from the traditional materials of poesy as Longfellow understood
them. Moreover, I know that there are many brave American men
who write about painful experiences. But what is special about
Whitman, what makes his diction remarkable in itself and fertile
for us today, is that he does all three of these things at once, and
in him they become a single act of creation. Unless we can see
the nobility of his courage, then we have neither the right nor
the intelligence to talk about the delicacy of his style.

Whitman's diction contains a lesson that can actually be learned,
and it does not require the vain imitation of his personal appearance and stylistic mannerisms. It is more spiritually inward than
any external accident can suggest. It is this: he deliberately seeks
in American life the occasions and persons who are central to
that life; he sometimes finds them harsh and violent, as in the
war; and he responds to the harshness with a huge effort of
imagination: to be delicate, precise, sensitive.

I realize that it is difficult to distinguish between the delicacy of Whitman's diction and his sensitivity as a man. But that is just the point. When a certain kind of diction, like a certain kind of meter, is employed by a coarse man, it automatically becomes a mannerism, or perhaps a stock device, detachable from the body of the poem, like a false eyelash, or a shapely artificial breast. Any concentration upon Whitman's stylistic mannerisms alone betrays an obsession with external, accidental things. Perhaps that is why so many bad poets have claimed Whitman as an ancestor.

I want also to say something about the delicacy of form in Whitman's poems. I think at once of the sentence in the 1855 Preface about rhythm and what he calls "uniformity." Here is the sentence again: "The rhythm and uniformity of perfect poems shows the free growth of metrical laws, and bud from them as unerringly and loosely as lilacs and roses on a bush, and take shapes as compact as the shapes of chestnuts and oranges."

This sentence can help us to understand what "form" meant to Whitman and also what it might mean to contemporary poets in America and elsewhere, if they have truly learned from Whitman and still wish to learn from him. The word "form" itself, however, may be ambiguous. So I will shun rhetorical definitions, which often threaten to mislead or oversimplify; and I will discuss a single short poem that, I believe, is a great poem because of the almost perfect delicacy of its form:

> I heard you solemn-sweet pipes of the organ as last Sunday
> mourn I pass'd the church,
> Winds of autumn, as I walk'd the woods at dusk I heard
> your long-stretch'd sighs up above so mournful,

I head the perfect Italian tenor singing at the opera, I heard
    the soprano in the midst of the quartet singing;
Heart of my love! you too I heard murmuring low through
    one of the wrists around my head,
Heard the pulse of you when all was still ringing little bells
    last night under my ear.

Does this poem have a form? If so, how can I describe it without losing in a general classification the very details that give the poem its life? I can think of at least two possibly helpful ways of answering these questions. First, Mr. Gay Wilson Allen (in his definitive biography of Whitman) supplies us with a crucial bit of textual information. The version of "I heard you solemn-sweet pipes" which I just quoted is not the only one. An earlier version, one of three poems which Whitman published in 1861, is quoted and discussed by Mr. Allen. The revisions are almost all deletions. The earlier version (printed in the New York *Leader,* October 12, 1861) contained apostrophes to "war-suggesting trumpets," to "you round-lipp'd cannons." In the version which Whitman apparently considered final (printed in the "Deathbed" edition of 1892), the references to war are deleted. Whitman also deleted a whole single line, in which he addresses a lady who played "delicious music on the harp."

What is left? A simple poem of five lines. Whitman addresses four different sounds. In these apostrophes and in his arrangement of them we can find the form of his poem.

The form is that of parallelism. But immediately we have to distinguish between the grammatical signification of "parallelism" and Whitman's actual use of it. A grammatical parallelism is primarily concerned with sentence-structure: noun balances noun,

verb balances verb, either as repetition or as antithesis. But in
Whitman's poem, the appearance of grammatical parallelism is
so rare as to be almost accidental. In fact, he almost seems to
avoid it. For he uses parallelism not as a device of repetition but
as an occasion for development. For this reason, we take a certain risk when we read "I heard you solemn-sweet pipes." After
the first two lines, we can know only two things: first, we cannot
hope to rest on mere parallel sentence-structure; second, the poet
is probably going to sing about another sound, but it might be
the sound of anything. (The possibility is a little scary in a
country where, for example, President Coolidge's taciturnity is
automaticaly considered a joke, instead of a great civic virtue.
Behind the uneasy joke lies the dreadful suspicion that we talk
too much.) There is no way to read Whitman's poem at all unless
we yield ourselves to its principle of growth, a principle that
reveals itself only in this particular poem, stage by stage.

Whitman first tries to make sure that we will not confuse his
poetic forms with the rules of grammar; and then he lets his
images grow, one out of another; and finally, we discover the
form of the poem as we read it, and we know what it is only
after we have finished.

It is this kind of formal growth that, I believe, gives special
appropriateness to Whitman's mention of "shapes as compact
as the shapes of chestnuts and oranges." These fruits do indeed
have "shapes"—delicate shapes indeed. And they are compact,
not diffuse. Their life depends on their form, which grows out
of the forms of blossoms, which in turn grew out of the forms
of trees, which in turn grew out of the forms of seeds. If I followed
the changes that overwhelm an orange seed, I should be startled

at the unexpected form of each stage of growth; but the form would be there nevertheless, however unexpected: at once un-dreamed-of and inevitable.

I have avoided the term "organic unity" because I wanted to read Whitman's poem afresh; and I am afraid that we might confuse the philosophical definition of a term in aesthetics with our empirical attempt to pay attention to the form of a poem. Just as bad poets tend to substitute the external accidents of Whitman's personal mannerisms and habits of dress for his poetry, so we readers might tend to substitute a general term for our reading of poetry—any poetry. If you mention the name of La-forgue, for example, it is a rare graduate student who will not immediately say, or think, the phrase "romantic irony," just as certain famous dogs helplessly salivated when a bell was rung. That's a good simile, as W. C. Fields once observed in another connection. Moreover, the simile is horrible; I wish I could make it even more so.

What is "form"? It is not simply the rules of grammar. And it cannot simply be equated with certain conventions of iambic verse. When reviewers of current American verse say that a certain poem is written "in form," they usually mean it is pre-dominantly iambic, either skillful or clumsy. But the form in Whitman's poems is not iambic. Form, in Whitman, is a prin-ciple of growth: one image or scene or sound *grows* out of an-other. The general device is parallelism, not of grammar but of action or some other meaning. Here is a further example of the parallel form, which is delicate and precise and therefore very powerful but which is not based on the repetition of the sentence-structure:

The little one sleeps in its cradle,
I lift the gauze and look a long time, and silently brush away
   flies with my hand.

The youngster and the red-faced girl turn aside up the bushy
   hill,
I peeringly view them from the top.

The suicide sprawls on the bloody floor of the bedroom,
I witness the corpse with its dabbled hair, I note where the
   pistol has fallen.

(Song of Myself, Section 8)

Form in Whitman is a principle of imagination: the proliferat-
ing of images out of one unifying vision. Every real poem has its
own form, which cannot be discovered through rhetoric, but only
through imagination. Whitman can teach current American poets
to destroy their own rhetoric and trust their own imagination.
I shudder to think what would happen if every current versifier in
America were to do that. (Is it a shudder of joy? A risky
question.)

I began by asking what Whitman has to do with us, and where
he is to be found. Some great writers of the past continue to
exist as objects of veneration and study. They are no less great
for all that. But Whitman is different, at least for us in America
today, scholars and poets alike. Of course he deserves veneration,
and he receives it. But he is also an immediate presence. He demands attention whether he is venerated or not. His work is
capable of exerting direct power upon some conventional divisions

in American life; and the power can heal the division. For example, in America today we still suffer from the conventional division between scholarly study of poetry on one hand and the attempt to practice the living art of poetry on the other. But consider Mr. Malcolm Cowley's 1959 reprinting of the first edition of *Leaves of Grass*. The reprinting is a work of the most careful scholarship: textual, historical, and biographical. It fully deserves the attention of scholars in the most dignified learned journals. It is respected by scholars who modestly accept their role as "academics"—men who labor faithfully by day at the scholarly profession, and are not especialy interested in reading current American verse during their evenings at home with their families. And yet . . . Mr. Cowley's reprinting of the 1855 *Leaves of Grass* is not only an act of sound scholarship; it is also an act of living poetry. I am sure that Mr. Cowley felt the relevance of Whitman's first edition to any lively interest in current American verse; but I doubt if he could have anticipated the effect of its living presence. The book itself is the newest poetry we have. It is as though the true spirit of Whitman had returned among us in order to rescue himself from the misinterpretations and abuses of his coarse imitators. He is, quite literally, living among us at this very moment; he has just published a new book; his poetry doesn't sound at all like the vast (too vast) clutter of work in two fairly representative anthologies of recent American verse: *The New Poets of England and America* (Meridian Books, 1957) and *The New American Poetry* (Grove Press, 1960). He is newer than both; he is precise, courageous, delicate, and seminal—an abundant poet. I think it would be entirely appropriate to award a prize to Whitman for a beautiful first book; and to Mr. Cowley for a revelation in which scholarship and thrilling poetic vitality are one and the same.

I think Whitman can also be found in other places, and I will mention two of them.

The delicate strength of Whitman was recognized and loved long ago by poets in the Spanish language. It is remarkable how often they speak of him. Often they speak of him in poems. I have in mind Federico García Lorca's magnificent "Ode to Walt Whitman," written in New York City at the end of the twenties. But the spirit of Whitman is everywhere present among Spanish and South American poets: in the form which rejects external rhetoric in order to discover and reveal a principle of growth; in the modesty and simplicity of diction; in the enormously courageous willingness to leap from one image into the unknown, in sheer faith that the next image will appear in the imagination; in the sensitive wholeness of the single poems which result from such imaginative courage; and, above all, in the belief in the imagination as the highest flowering of human life (the phrase belongs to Jorge Guillén), not just a rhetorical ornament. These are all powers of Whitman's spirit. They have been enlivening Spanish poetry for at least fifty years.

Moreover, we are in the midst of a wave of translation in the United States. The September, 1961, issue of *Poetry* (Chicago) is entirely devoted to translation. The poems of Pablo Neruda of Chile, César Vallejo of Peru, and of several great writers from Spain—Juan Ramón Jiménez, Antonio Machado, Jorge Guillén, Miguel Hernandez, and Blas de Otero, to name only a few—are being not only read but also translated by several American writers, and this effort cannot help but lead to Whitman. It is sometimes said that the true spirit of Poe was absorbed into contemporary American literature only after Poe had been truly understood by the French. Perhaps the true Whitman may return to the United States from Spain and South America "through the sky that is below the ground" (Jiménez).

We have spirits capable of welcoming him. Louis Simpson's imagination is obsessed with the most painful details of current American life, which he reveals under a very powerfully developed sense of American history. Several of his latest poems directly address Whitman as a figure who discovers that the Open Road has led to the barren Pacific, to the used-car graveyard, to the earthly paradise of the real-estate agents. Mr. Simpson describes America and Americans in a vision totally free from advertising and propaganda, just as Whitman described the Civil War soldiers, not as "Our Boys" or such like, but rather as startled white faces of youths shot in the abdomen.

Robert Bly's Whitmanesque powers include the ability to write about what he calls "the dark figures of politics." A remarkable sequence describing such "figures" is *Poems for the Ascension of J. P. Morgan*, published in *New World Writing #15*. I want to quote a new poem of Bly's. It is called "After the Industrial Revolution, All Things Happen at Once."

> Now we enter a strange world, where the Hessian Christmas
> Still goes on, and Washington has not reached the other shore;
> The Whiskey Boys
> Are gathering again on the meadows of Pennsylvania
> And the Republic is still sailing on the open sea.

In 1956 I saw a black angel in Washington, dancing
On a barge, saying, Let us now divide kennel dogs
And hunting dogs; Henry Cabot Lodge, in New York,
Talking of sugar cane in Cuba; Ford,
In Detroit, drinking mothers' milk;
Ford, saying, "History is bunk!"
And Wilson saying, "What is good for General Motors—"

Who is it, singing? Don't you hear singing?
It is the dead of Cripple Creek;
Coxey's army
Like turkeys are singing from the tops of trees!
And the Whiskey Boys are drunk outside Philadelphia.

Denise Levertov, an extremely gifted poet, suggests Whitman
in several ways: her reverence for the civilization of the past, so
deep as to be utterly modest; her willingness to discover the new
forms of her imagination; and her nobility of spirit, which knows
what is worthy of celebration and is capable of great moral understanding. Two of her recent poems (included in her superb book
from New Directions, *The Jacob's Ladder*), "In Memory of Boris
Pasternak" and "During the Eichmann Trial," embody this
nobility perfectly. The latter sequence includes a cry of pity for
Adolf Eichmann; and Miss Levertov sees everyone in the twen-
tieth century caught and exposed in Eichmann's glass cage. The
subject is almost unendurably horrible; and it is treated with
a tenderness which is in itself an imaginative strength of great
purity.

So Whitman is alive; in person, with his own poems; in spirit,
among the Spanish writers who long ago understood him; and

among certain American writers, in their translations and in their own spiritual courage. Whitman has delicacy; moreover, he dared to subject his delicacy to the tests of the real world, both the external world of nineteenth-century America, with its wars and loud cities and buffaloes vanishing into herds of clouds, and the inner world of his spirit. He loved the human body, he knew that when you kill a man he dies, and he exposed his feelings to the coarsest of wars in order to record its truth. He had nothing against British literature; but he felt that Americans have even greater stores of imagination to draw upon. Here are some of his words, from *Collect: Notes Left Over:*

> I strongly recommend all the young men and young women of the United States to whom it may be eligible, to overhaul the well-freighted fleets, the literature of Italy, Spain, France, Germany, so full of those elements of freedom, self-possession, gay-heartedness, subtlety, dilation, needed in preparations for the future of the States. I only wish we could have really good translations. I rejoice at the feeling for Oriental researches and poetry, and hope it will continue.

The man who wrote those words was not only a very great poet. He was also a generous human being, and he rejoiced in the hopes of his fellows. I believe that American poetry at this moment is able to show itself worthy of Whitman's intelligence, his courage, his supremely delicate imagination. At any rate, many living American poets cherish Whitman's best powers; and one cannot love such things without being inwardly changed. We honor Whitman; and we share the happy thought that he would have been delighted and would have wanted to honor us

in return. Surely he would have loved another new American
poem which occurs to me, for it speaks with his own best voice
—uncluttered, courageous, and kind. The poem is Mr. David
Ignatow's "Walt Whitman in the Civil War Hospitals," which
I quote in its entirety:

> Prescient, my hands soothing
> their foreheads, by my love
> I earn them. In their presence
> I am wretched as death. They smile
> to me of love. They cheer me
> and I smile. These are stones
> in the catapulting world;
> they fly, bury themselves in flesh,
> in a wall, in earth; in midair
> break against each other
> and are without sound.
> I sent them catapulting.
> They outflew my voice
> towards vacant spaces,
> but I have called them farther,
> to the stillness beyond,
> to death which I have praised.

APPENDIX

APPENDIX

Versions of "Out of the Cradle Endlessly Rocking"

Three versions of this poem can be distinguished; two of them appear on facing pages following this note. The poem was printed first as "A Child's Reminiscence" in the New York *Saturday Press* (edited by Henry Clapp, Jr., and Robert R. Pearsall) for December 24, 1859. A second version was included the following year as "A Word Out of the Sea" in the 1860 edition of *Leaves of Grass*. Most of the changes that the poem later underwent were introduced by Whitman in the 1867 edition of *Leaves of Grass*. However, the final and familiar title, "Out of the Cradle Endlessly Rocking," was not used until 1871; and a few major emendations —most notably, the deletion of almost the whole of the former section 31 of "Reminiscence" and the addition of the present line 182—were made in the edition of 1881. The third and final version, therefore, can be said to be that of 1881.

As between the first (1859) and the second (1860) versions, apart from the suggestive shift of title, several differences are worth mentioning. The lines prior to the "Reminiscence" carried the title "PRE-VERSE" in 1859; and that section initially concluded as follows:

Throwing myself on the sand, I
Confronting the waves, sing.

In "Reminiscence § 1," the line "When the snows had melted, and the Fifth Month grass was growing" was added in 1860; while the phrase "close by the shore" was dropped from the original third line of "Reminiscence § 7." Interestingly enough, the entire "song" of the bereaved bird remained untouched (except for a trifling two-word deletion from § 21) from the first to the second version. The parenthetical remark in § 32—"(for I will conquer it)"—was added in 1860; and so was the phrase "the word up from the waves" in the final section. Most of the other changes (I have counted twenty-eight items in all) are relatively trifling—deletions of single words or small groups of words, emendations of spelling (e.g., "clew" for "clue") or of punctuation and typography ("two together," in the final section, for *Two Together*). The 1859 version, meanwhile, may be examined in the volume edited by Thomas O. Mabbott and Rollo G. Silver, University of Washington Quartos, No. 1 (Seattle, 1930), a volume that also contains, among other things, a contemptuous dismissal of "A Child's Reminiscence" and of Whitman in general, in an article that appeared in the Cincinnati *Daily Commerical* on December 28, 1859, was reprinted in the *Saturday Press* on January 7, 1860, and was answered in a warm, unsigned piece by Whitman himself in that same issue.

A WORD OUT OF THE SEA
(*Leaves of Grass,* Boston, 1860, pp. 269–77)

Out of the rocked cradle,
Out of the mocking-bird's throat, the musical shuttle,
Out of the boy's mother's womb, and from the nipples of her breasts,
Out of the Ninth Month midnight,
Over the sterile sands, and the fields beyond, where the child, leaving his
    bed, wandered alone, bare-headed, barefoot,
Down from the showered halo,
Up from the mystic play of shadows, twining and twisting as if they were
    alive,
Out from the patches of briers and blackberries,
From the memories of the bird that chanted to me,
From your memories, sad brother—from the fitful risings and fallings
    I heard,
From under that yellow half-moon, late-risen, and swollen as if with tears,
From those beginning notes of sickness and love, there in the transparent
    mist,
From the thousand responses of my heart, never to cease,
From the myriad thence-aroused words,
From the word stronger and more delicious than any,
From such, as now they start, the scene revisiting,
As a flock, twittering, rising, or overheard passing,
Borne hither—ere all eludes me, hurriedly,
A man—yet by these tears a little boy again,
Throwing myself on the sand, confronting the waves,
I, chanter of pains and joys, uniter of here and hereafter,
Taking all hints to use them—but swiftly leaping beyond them,
A reminiscence sing.

REMINISCENCE

1. Once, Paumanok,
    When the snows had melted, and the Fifth Month grass was growing,
    Up this sea-shore, in some briers,
    Two guests from Alabama—two together,
    And their nest, and four light-green eggs, spotted with brown,
    And every day the he-bird, to and fro, near at hand,
    And every day the she-bird, crouched on her nest, silent, with bright
    eyes,

OUT OF THE CRADLE ENDLESSLY ROCKING
Final Version (1881)

Out of the cradle endlessly rocking,
Out of the mocking-bird's throat, the musical shuttle,
Out of the Ninth-month midnight,
Over the sterile sands and the fields beyond, where the child leaving
    his bed wander'd alone, bareheaded, barefoot,
Down from the shower'd halo,   5
Up from the mystic play of shadows twining and twisting as if they
    were alive,
Out from the patches of briers and blackberries,
From the memories of the bird that chanted to me,
From your memories sad brother, from the fitful risings and fallings I
    heard,
From under that yellow half-moon late-risen and swollen as if with
    tears,   10
From those beginning notes of yearning and love there in the mist,
From the thousand responses of my heart never to cease,
From the myriad thence-arous'd words,
From the word stronger and more delicious than any,
From such as now they start the scene revisiting,   15
As a flock, twittering, rising, or overhead passing,
Borne hither, ere all eludes me, hurriedly,
A man, yet by these tears a little boy again,
Throwing myself on the sand, confronting the waves,
I, chanter of pains and joys, uniter of here and hereafter,   20
Taking all hints to use them, but swiftly leaping beyond them,
A reminiscence sing.

Once Paumanok,
When the lilac-scent was in the air and Fifth-month grass was growing,
Up this seashore in some briers,   25
Two feather'd guests from Alabama, two together,
And their nest, and four light-green eggs spotted with brown,
And every day the he-bird to and fro near at hand,
And every day the she-bird crouch'd on her nest, silent, with bright eyes,

And every day I, a curious boy, never too close, never disturbing them,
Cautiously peering, absorbing, translating.

2. *Shine! Shine!*
   Pour down your warmth, great Sun!
   While we bask—we two together.

3. *Two together!*
   Winds blow South, or winds blow North,
   Day come white, or night come black,
   Home, or rivers and mountains from home,
   Singing all time, minding no time,
   If we two but keep together.

4. Till of a sudden,
   May-be killed, unknown to her mate,
   One forenoon the she-bird crouched not on the nest,
   Nor returned that afternoon, nor the next,
   Nor ever appeared again.

5. And thenceforward, all summer, in the sound of the sea,
   And at night, under the full of the moon, in calmer weather,
   Over the hoarse surging of the sea,
   Or flitting from brier to brier by day,
   I saw, I heard at intervals, the remaining one, the he-bird,
   The solitary guest from Alabama.

6. *Blow! Blow!*
   Blow up sea-winds along Paumanok's shore;
   I wait and I wait, till you blow my mate to me.

7. Yes, when the stars glistened,
   All night long, on the prong of a moss-scallop'd stake,
   Down, almost amid the slapping waves,
   Sat the lone singer, wonderful, causing tears.

8. He called on his mate,
   He poured forth the meanings which I, of all men, know.

9. Yes, my brother, I know,
   The rest might not—but I have treasured every note,

And every day I, a curious boy, never too close, never disturbing them,   30
Cautiously peering, absorbing, translating.

Shine! shine! shine!
Pour down your warmth, great sun!
While we bask, we two together.
Two together!   35
Winds blow south, or winds blow north,
Day come white, or night come black,
Home, or rivers and mountains from home,
Singing all time, minding no time,
While we two keep together.   40

Till of a sudden,
May-be kill'd, unknown to her mate,
One forenoon the she-bird crouch'd not on the nest,
Nor return'd that afternoon, nor the next,
Nor ever appear'd again.   45

And thenceforward all summer in the sound of the sea,
And at night under the full of the moon in calmer weather,
Over the hoarse surging of the sea,
Or flitting from brier to brier by day,
I saw, I heard at intervals the remaining one, the he-bird,   50
The solitary guest from Alabama.

Blow! blow! blow!
Blow up sea-winds along Paumanok's shore;
I wait and I wait till you blow my mate to me.

Yes, when the stars glisten'd,   55
All night long on the prong of a moss-scallop'd stake,
Down almost amid the slapping waves,
Sat the lone singer wonderful causing tears.

He call'd on his mate,
He pour'd forth the meanings which I of all men know.   60

Yes my brother I know,
The rest might not, but I have treasur'd every note,

For once, and more than once, dimly, down to the beach gliding,
Silent, avoiding the moonbeams, blending myself with the shadows,
Recalling now the obscure shapes, the echoes, the sounds and sights
    after their sorts,
The white arms out in the breakers tirelessly tossing,
I, with bare feet, a child, the wind wafting my hair,
Listened long and long.

10. Listened, to keep, to sing—now translating the notes,
    Following you, my brother.

11. *Soothe! Soothe!*
    Close on its wave soothes the wave behind,
    And again another behind, embracing and lapping, every one close,
    But my love soothes not me.

12. *Low hangs the moon—it rose late,*
    O it is lagging—O I think it is heavy with love.

13. *O madly the sea pushes upon the land,*
    With love—with love.

14. *O night!*
    O do I not see my love fluttering out there among the breakers?
    What is that little black thing I see there in the white?

15. *Loud! Loud!*
    Loud I call to you my love!
    High and clear I shoot my voice over the waves,
    Surely you must know who is here,
    You must know who I am, my love.

16. *Low-hanging moon!*
    What is that dusky spot in your brown yellow?
    O it is the shape of my mate!
    O moon, do not keep her from me any longer.

17. *Land! O land!*
    Whichever way I turn, O I think you could give me my mate back
      again, if you would,
    For I am almost sure I see her dimly whichever way I look.

For more than once dimly down to the beach gliding,
Silent, avoiding the moonbeams, blending myself with the shadows,
Recalling now the obscure shapes, the echoes, the sounds and sights
    after their sorts,   65
The white arms out in the breakers tirelessly tossing,
I, with bare feet, a child, the wind wafting my hair,
Listen'd long and long.

Listen'd to keep, to sing, now translating the notes,
Following you my brother.   70

Soothe! soothe! soothe!
Close on its wave soothes the wave behind,
And again another behind embracing and lapping, every one close,
But my love soothes not me, not me.

Low hangs the moon, it rose late,   75
It is lagging—O I think it is heavy with love, with love.

O madly the sea pushes upon the land,
With love, with love.

O night! do I not see my love fluttering out among the breakers?
What is that little black thing I see there in the white?   80

Loud! loud! loud!
Loud I call to you, my love!
High and clear I shoot my voice over the waves,
Surely you must know who is here, is here,
You must know who I am, my love.   85

Low-hanging moon!
What is that dusky spot in your brown yellow?
O it is the shape, the shape of my mate!
O moon do not keep her from me any longer.

Land! land! O land!   90
Whichever way I turn, O I think you could give me my mate back
    again if you only would,
For I am almost sure I see her dimly whichever way I look.

18. *O rising stars!*
    Perhaps the one I want so much will rise with some of you.

19. *O throat!*
    Sound clearer through the atmosphere!
    Pierce the woods, the earth,
    Somewhere listening to catch you must be the one I want.

20. *Shake out, carols!*
    Solitary here—the night's carols!
    Carols of lonesome love! Death's carols!
    Carols under that lagging, yellow, waning moon!
    O, under that moon, where she droops almost down into the sea!
    O reckless, despairing carols.

21. *But soft!*
    Sink low—soft!
    Soft! Let me just murmur,
    And do you wait a moment, you husky-noised sea,
    For somewhere I believe I heard my mate responding to me,
    So faint—I must be still to listen,
    But not altogether still, for then she might not come immediately to me.

22. *Hither, my love!*
    Here I am! Here!
    With this just-sustained note I announce myself to you,
    This gentle call is for you, my love.

23. *Do not be decoyed elsewhere!*
    That is the whistle of the wind—it is not my voice,
    That is the fluttering of the spray,
    Those are the shadows of leaves.

24. *O darkness! O in vain!*
    O I am very sick and sorrowful.

25. *O brown halo in the sky, near the moon, dropping upon the sea!*
    O troubled reflection in the sea!
    O throat! O throbbing heart!
    O all—and I singing uselessly all the night.

O rising stars!
Perhaps the one I want so much will rise, will rise with some of you.

O throat! O trembling throat!   95
Sound clearer through the atmosphere!
Pierce the woods, the earth,
Somewhere listening to catch you must be the one I want.

Shake out carols!
Solitary here, the night's carols!   100
Carols of lonesome love! death's carols!
Carols under that lagging, yellow, waning moon!
O under that moon where she droops almost down into the sea!
O reckless despairing carols.

But soft! sink low!   105
Soft! let me just murmur,
And do you wait a moment you husky-nois'd sea,
For somewhere I believe I heard my mate responding to me,
So faint, I must be still, be still to listen,
But not altogether still, for then she might not come immediately to
*   me.*   110

Hither my love!
Here I am! here!
With this just-sustain'd note I announce myself to you,
This gentle call is for you my love, for you.

Do not be decoy'd elsewhere,   115
That is the whistle of the wind, it is not my voice,
That is the fluttering, the fluttering of the spray,
Those are the shadows of leaves.

O darkness! O in vain!
O I am very sick and sorrowful.   120

O brown halo in the sky near the moon, drooping upon the sea!
O troubled reflection in the sea!
O throat! O throbbing heart!
And I singing uselessly, uselessly all the night.

26. *Murmur! Murmur on!*
    O murmurs—you yourselves make me continue to sing, I know not
    why.

27. *O past! O joy!*
    In the air—in the woods—over fields,
    Loved! Loved! Loved! Loved! Loved!
    Loved—but no more with me,
    We two together no more.

28. The aria sinking,
    All else continuing—the stars shining,
    The winds blowing—the notes of the wondrous bird echoing,
    With angry moans the fierce old mother yet, as ever, incessantly
        moaning,
    On the sands of Paumanok's shore gray and rustling,
    The yellow half-moon, enlarged, sagging down, drooping, the face of
        the sea almost touching,
    The boy extatic—with his bare feet the waves, with his hair the
        atmosphere dallying,
    The love in the heart pent, now loose, now at last tumultuously burst-
        ing,
    The aria's meaning, the ears, the Soul, swiftly depositing,
    The strange tears down the cheeks coursing,
    The colloquy there—the trio—each uttering,
    The undertone—the savage old mother, incessantly crying,
    To the boy's Soul's questions sullenly timing—some drowned secret
        hissing,
    To the outsetting bard of love.

29. Bird! (then said the boy's Soul),
    Is it indeed toward your mate you sing? or is it mostly to me?
    For I that was a child, my tongue's use sleeping,
    Now that I have heard you,
    Now in a moment I know what I am for—I awake,
    And already a thousand singers—a thousand songs, clearer, louder,
        more sorrowful than yours,
    A thousand warbling echoes have started to life within me,
    Never to die.

30. O throes!
    O you demon, singing by yourself—projecting me,

O past! O happy life! O songs of joy!   125
In the air, in the woods, over fields,
Loved! loved! loved! loved! loved!
But my mate no more, no more with me!
We two together no more.

The aria sinking,   130
All else continuing, the stars shining,
The winds blowing, the notes of the bird continuous echoing,
With angry moans the fierce old mother incessantly moaning,
On the sands of Paumanok's shore gray and rustling,
The yellow half-moon enlarged, sagging down, drooping, the face of
   the sea almost touching,   135
The boy ecstatic, with his bare feet the waves, with his hair the atmosphere
   dallying,
The love in the heart long pent, now loose, now at last tumultuously
   bursting,
The aria's meaning, the ears, the soul, swiftly depositing,
The strange tears down the cheeks coursing,
The colloquy there, the trio, each uttering,   140
The undertone, the savage old mother incessantly crying,
To the boy's soul's questions sullenly timing, some drown'd secret hissing,
To the outsetting bard.

Demon or bird! (said the boy's soul,)
Is it indeed toward your mate you sing? or is it really to me?   145
For I, that was a child, my tongue's use sleeping, now I have heard you,
Now in a moment I know what I am for, I awake,
And already a thousand singers, a thousand songs, clearer, louder and
   more sorrowful than yours,
A thousand warbling echoes have started to life within me, never to die.

O you singer solitary, singing by yourself, projecting me,   150

O solitary me, listening—never more shall I cease imitating, per-
petuating you,
Never more shall I escape,
Never more shall the reverberations,
Never more the cries of unsatisfied love be absent from me,
Never again leave me to be the peaceful child I was before what
there, in the night,
By the sea, under the yellow and sagging moon,
The dusky demon aroused—the fire, the sweet hell within,
The unknown want, the destiny of me.

31. O give me some clew!
O if I am to have so much, let me have more!
O a word! O what is my destination?
O I fear it is henceforth chaos!
O how joys, dreads, convolutions, human shapes, and all shapes,
spring as from graves around me!
O phantoms! you cover all the land, and all the sea!
O I cannot see in the dimness whether you smile or frown upon me;
O vapor, a look, a word! O well-beloved!
O you dear women's and men's phantoms!

32. A word then, (for I will conquer it,)
The word final, superior to all,
Subtle, sent up—what is it? I listen;
Are you whispering it, and have been all the time, you sea-waves?
Is that it from your liquid rims and wet sands?

33. Answering, the sea,
Delaying not, hurrying not,
Whispered me through the night, and very plainly before daybreak,
Lisped to me constantly the low and delicious word Death,
And again Death—ever Death, Death, Death,
Hissing melodious, neither like the bird, nor like my aroused child's
heart,
But edging near, as privately for me, rustling at my feet,
And creeping thence steadily up to my ears,
Death, Death, Death, Death, Death.

34. Which I do not forget,
But fuse the song of two together,

O solitary me listening, never more shall I cease perpetuating you,
Never more shall I escape, never more the reverberations,
Never more the cries of unsatisfied love be absent from me,
Never again leave me to be the peaceful child I was before what there
    in the night,
By the sea under the yellow and sagging moon,   155
The messenger there arous'd, the fire, the sweet hell within,
The unknown want, the destiny of me.

O give me the clew! (it lurks in the night here somewhere,)
O if I am to have so much, let me have more!

A word then, (for I will conquer it,)   160
The word final, superior to all,
Subtle, sent up—what is it? I listen;
Are you whispering it, and have been all the time, you sea waves?
Is that it from your liquid rims and wet sands?

Whereto answering, the sea,   165
Delaying not, hurrying not,
Whisper'd me through the night, and very plainly before daybreak,
Lisp'd to me the low and delicious word death,
And again death, death, death, death,
Hissing melodious, neither like the bird nor like my arous'd child's
    heart,   170
But edging near as privately for me rustling at my feet,
Creeping thence steadily up to my ears and laving me softly all over
Death, death, death, death, death.

Which I do not forget,
But fuse the song of my dusky demon and brother,   175

That was sung to me in the moonlight on Paumanok's gray beach,
With the thousand responsive songs, at random,
My own songs, awaked from that hour,
And with them the key, the word up from the waves,
The word of the sweetest song, and all songs,
That strong and delicious word which, creeping to my feet,
The sea whispered me.

That he sang to me in the moonlight on Paumanok's gray beach,
With the thousand responsive songs at random,
My own songs awaked from that hour,
And with them the key, the word up from the waves,
The word of the sweetest song and all songs,   180
That strong and delicious word which, creeping to my feet,
(Or like some old crone rocking the cradle, swathed in sweet garments,
    bending aside,)
The sea whisper'd me.

BIBLIOGRAPHY OF WORKS CITED

Abrams, Meyer H. *The Mirror and the Lamp.* New York, 1953.

Allen, Gay Wilson. *The Solitary Singer.* New York, 1955.

—— *Walt Whitman Handbook.* New York, 1946.

Asselineau, Roger. *L'evolution de Walt Whitman après la première édition des Feuilles d'Herbe.* Paris, 1956. Part I translated into English as *The Evolution of Walt Whitman.* Cambridge, Mass., 1960.

Bowers, Fredson. *Whitman's Manuscripts: Leaves of Grass (1860).* Chicago, 1955.

Catel, Jean. *Walt Whitman: la naissance du poète.* Paris, 1929.

Chase, Richard. *The American Novel and Its Tradition.* New York, 1957.

—— *Walt Whitman Reconsidered.* New York, 1955.

Cowley, Malcolm, ed. *Walt Whitman's Leaves of Grass: The First (1855) Edition.* New York, 1959.

Cox, James M. "Walt Whitman, Mark Twain, and the Civil War," *Sewanee Review,* LXIX (Spring, 1961), 185–204.

Faner, Robert D. *Walt Whitman and Opera.* Philadelphia, 1951.

Feidelson, Charles, Jr. *Symbolism and American Literature.* Chicago, 1953.

Fiedler, Leslie A., ed. *Whitman.* Laurel Paperback, New York, 1959.

Frye, Northrop. *Anatomy of Criticism.* Princeton, N.J., 1957.

Jarrell, Randall. *Poetry and the Age.* New York, 1953.

Lawrence, D. H. *Studies in Classic American Literature.* New York, 1953.

Matthiessen, F. O. *American Renaissance.* New York, 1941.

Miller, James E., Jr. *A Critical Guide to Leaves of Grass.* Chicago, 1957.

Miller, James E., Jr., Karl Shapiro, and Bernice Slote. *Start with the Sun.* Lincoln, Nebraska, 1960.

Pearce, Roy Harvey, ed. *Leaves of Grass by Walt Whitman: Facsimile Edition of the 1860 Text.* Ithaca, New York, 1961.

Rourke, Constance. *American Humor: A Study of the National Character.* New York, 1931.

Schyberg, Frederik. *Walt Whitman.* Copenhagen, 1933. Trans. Evie Allison Allen. New York, 1951.

Shapiro, Karl. *See* Miller, James E., Jr.

Slote, Bernice. *See* Miller, James E., Jr.

Stovall, Floyd. "Main Drifts in Whitman's Poetry," *American Literature,* IV (1932), 3–21.

THE PROGRAM

September 5 through September 8, 1961

CONFERENCES

I VICTORIAN CRITICISM
 Directed by Bernard Schilling, University of Rochester
 1 THE VICTORIAN SENSIBILITY
 William A. Madden, Indiana University
 2 JOHN RUSKIN
 Gabriele Bernhard, Yale University
 3 ARNOLD'S HUMANISM: POETRY AS A CRITICISM OF LIFE
 Wayne Shumaker, University of California at Berkeley
 4 GEORGE SAINTSBURY
 René Wellek, Yale University

II THE PREVALENCE OF WALT WHITMAN
 Directed by Lewis Leary, Columbia University
 1 WHITMAN, POUND, AND THE PROSE TRADITION
 Samuel Hynes, Swarthmore College
 2 THE ARCHITECTURE OF *The Bridge*
 John E. Unterecker, Columbia University
 3 WHITMAN AND THOMAS: THE YAWP AND THE GAB
 James E. Miller, Jr., University of Nebraska
 4 THE DELICACY OF WALT WHITMAN
 James A. Wright, University of Minnesota

III   TRAVEL LITERATURE
       Directed by Warner G. Rice, University of Michigan
       1 "OUR MEMORY SEES MORE THAN OUR EYES":
       EIGHTEENTH-CENTURY TRAVEL LITERATURE
       George Kahrl, Elmira College
       2 ELEMENTS OF CONVENTION AND NOVELTY IN THE ROMANTIC
       GENERATION'S EXPERIENCE OF ITALY
       Herbert Barrows, University of Michigan
       3 TRAVEL LITERATURE AND THE MODE OF ROMANCE IN THE
       RENAISSANCE
       W. T. Jewkes, Pennsylvania State University

IV   LITERATURE AND THE VISUAL ARTS
       Directed by Jean H. Hagstrum, Northwestern University
       1 NARRATIVE TECHNIQUE IN THE VISUAL ARTS AND IN CHAUCER
       Curt Zimansky, University of Iowa
       2 THE UNION OF THE ARTS IN WILLIAM BLAKE
       Jean Hagstrum, Northwestern University
       3 GOTHIC VERSUS RENAISSANCE: MORRIS AND BROWNING
       Wylie Sypher, Simmons College

Ruth M. Adams, Douglass College; Gellert Alleman, Newark College of Arts and Sciences, Rutgers University; Robert J. Allen, Williams College; Marcia Allentuck, City College of New York; Lynn Altenbernd, University of Illinois; Reta Anderson, Woman's College, University of North Carolina; Sister Anne Cyril, Emmanuel College; Sister Aquin Lally, B.V.M., Mundelein College; Sister Mary Arthur, O.P., College of St. Mary of the Springs; Robert W. Ayers, Georgetown University; C. L. Barber, Amherst College; Herbert Barrows, University of Michigan; Mary P. Barrows, University of California; Lynn C. Bartlett, Vassar College; Phyllis Bartlett, Queens College; Warren Beck, Lawrence College; D. W. Becker, Miami University; Frances H. Bennett, Ohio Northern University; Alice R. Bensen, Eastern Michigan College; Lia Beretta, Mary Washington College; Whitney Blake, Oxford University Press; Max Bluestone, Babson Institute; Edward Bostetter, University of Washington; Edwin T. Bowden, University of Texas; Brother C. Francis Bowers, Manhattan College; the Reverend John D. Boyd, Fordham University; Margaret M. Bryant, Brooklyn College; Jean R. Buchert, Woman's College, University of North Carolina; Brother Fidelean Burke, F.S.C., La Salle College; Kathleen Byrne, Seton Hill College.

Grace Calder, Hunter College; Kenneth N. Cameron, The Carl H. Pforzheimer Library; Norman Carlson, DePauw University; Albert H. Carter, Florida Presbyterian College; Sister Catherine Regina, College of Mount Saint Vincent; Sister Mary Charles, I.H.M., Immaculata College; Hugh C. G. Chase (Milton, Massachusetts); John A. Christie, Vassar College; Sister Mary Chrysostom, College of Mount Saint Vincent; James L. Clifford, Columbia University; Lester Conner, Columbia University; Allen B. Cook, United States Naval Academy; John S. Coolidge, University of California at Berkeley; Lucille Crighton, Gulf Park College; James Croushore, Mary Washington College; Eileen H. Curran, Colby College; Kenneth Curry, University of Tennessee; Curtis Dahl, Wheaton College; Elizabeth Daniels, Vassar College; Charles T. Davis, Pennsylvania State University; Richard Beale Davis, University of Tennessee; Winifred M. Davis, The Carl H. Pforzheimer Library; Charlotte D'Evelyn, Mount Holyoke College; Agnes Donahue, Barat College; Edward Easton, Pace College; Ursula Eder, Brooklyn College; Sister Elizabeth Marian, College of Mount Saint Vincent; Scott Elledge, Carleton College; Richard Ellmann, Northwestern University; Martha England, Queens College; David Erdman, New York Public Library; Sister Marie Eugenie, i.h.m., Immaculata College; Robert O. Evans, University of Kentucky.

H. Alfred Farrell, Lincoln University; Alice M. Farrison, North Carolina College at Durham; W. Edward Farrison, North Carolina College at Durham; Arthur Fenner, Catholic University; Joseph Firebaugh, Flint College of the University of Michigan; Edward G. Fletcher, University of Texas; F. Cudworth Flint, Dartmouth College; George H. Ford, University of Rochester; Elizabeth Foster, Oberlin College; Frances A. Foster, Vassar College; Sister Mary Francis, College of Mount Saint Vincent; W. M. Frohock, Harvard University; Ligeia Gallagher, Loyola University; Edward L. Galligan, Western Michigan University; Harold Garriott, DePauw University; John Gassner, Yale University; Helmut E. Gerber, Purdue University; Walker Gibson, New York University; Richard Gollin, University of Rochester; Sister Mary Gonzaga, r.s.m., Convent of Mercy (Albany, New York); Sandra Kay Gowl, Mary Washington College; the Reverend Thomas Grace, Holy Cross College; John E. Grant, University of Connecticut; James Gray, Bishop's University; Helen T. Greany, Columbia University.

J. H. Hagstrum, Northwestern University; V. B. Halpert, Polytechnic Institute of Brooklyn; Robert Halsband, Columbia University; Victor M. Hamm, Marquette University; Katharine S. Harris, Queens College; John A. Hart, Carnegie Institute of Technology; Ann Louise Hayes, Carnegie Institute of Technology; A. T. Hazen, Columbia University; Miriam M. Heffernan, Brooklyn College; Thelma J. Henner, Columbia University; the Reverend William B. Hill, s.j., Novitiate of St. Isaac Jogues; Frederick W. Hilles, Yale University; C. Fenno Hoffman, Jr., Massachusetts Institute of Technology; Stanley M. Holberg, St. Lawrence University; Vivian C. Hopkins, State University of New York; John Dixon Hunt, Vassar College; Eleanor C. Jared, Huron College; W. T. Jewkes, Pennsylvania State University; Sister Mary Joannes, r.s.m., Mercy College; George W. Johnson, Temple University; S. F. Johnson, Columbia University; Sister Joseph Mary, Emmanuel College; George M. Kahrl, Elmira College; Stanley J. Kahrl, Harvard University; R. J. Kaufman, University of Rochester; Norman Kelvin, City College of New York; James E. Kennedy, Upsala College; Edith Kern, Coe College; Karl Kiralis, St. Lawrence University; Clara M. Kirk, Douglass College; Carl F. Klinck, University of Western Ontario; Henry Knepler, Illinois Institute of Technology; Frank Krutzke, Colorado College; George Kummer, Western Reserve University.

James Craig LaDrière, Catholic University; the Reverend John P. Lahey, s.j., Le Moyne College; Seymour Lainoff, Yeshiva College; the Reverend Henry St. C. Lavin, s.j., Loyola College (Baltimore); Lewis Leary, Columbia University; Jean S. Lindsay (Shrewsbury, New Jersey); Winslow H. Loveland (Hyde Park, Massachusetts); Joseph P. Lovering, Canisius College; Marion K. Mabey, Connecticut College; Charles J. McCann, Canisius College; John McChesney, Hotchkiss School; Julia McGrew, Vassar College; Maynard Mack, Yale University; Richard Macksey, Johns Hopkins University; Elizabeth McLaughlin, Bucknell University; Kenneth MacLean, Victoria College, University of Toronto; William Madden, Indiana University; Gerhard Magnus, Philadelphia Museum College of Art; Mother C. E. Maguire, Newton College of the Sacred Heart;

Leonard Manheim, City College of New York; the Reverend Frederick Manion, s.j., Xavier University; Harold C. Martin, Harvard University; Louis Martz, Yale University; Donald C. Mell, Rutgers University; Vivian H. S. Mercier, City College of New York; Harrison T. Meserole, Pennsylvania State University; John H. Middendorf, Columbia University; James E. Miller, Jr., University of Nebraska; Ralph N. Miller, Western Michigan University; Francis E. Mineka, Cornell University; Louie M. Miner (Brooklyn, New York); Mother Grace Monahan, o.s.u., College of New Rochelle; S. G. Mullins, Laval University; Howard M. Munford, Middlebury College; William Nelson, Columbia University; Pauline Newton, North Carolina College at Durham; Eleanor L. Nicholes, Harvard University; the Reverend William T. Noon, s.j., Loyola Seminary; Gertrude E. Noyes, Connecticut College.

W. H. Sterg O'Dell, Drexel Institute of Technology; Mother Eileen O'Gorman, Manhattanville College of the Sacred Heart; the Reverend Joseph E. O'Neill, s.j., Fordham University; Ants Oras, University of Florida; James M. Osborn, Yale University; Stephen C. Paine, Salem College; John W. Parker, Fayetteville State Teachers College (North Carolina); Coleman O. Parsons, City College of New York; Sister Mary Paton (Ryan), r.s.m., Saint Xavier College; Sister Marie Paula, College of Mount Saint Vincent; Norman Holmes Pearson, Yale University; William Peery, Tulane University; Margaret I. Pfau, Elmira College; Henry Popkin, New York University; Abbie F. Potts, Rockford College; Lacy Powell, Mary Washington College; Robert Preyer, Brandeis University; Hereward T. Price, University of Michigan; Max Putzel, University of Connecticut; the Reverend C. J. Quirk, s.j., Loyola University of the South; Paul Ramsey, Elmira College; Warren Ramsey, University of California at Berkeley; Helen Randall, Smith College; Charles Ray, North Carolina College at Durham; John K. Reeves, Skidmore College; Elizabeth Revell, Huron College of University of Western Ontario; Warner G. Rice, University of Michigan; Josephine G. Rickard, Houghton College; Sister M. Rita Margaret, o.p., Caldwell College for Women; Leo Rockes, Rochester Institute of Technology;

Francis X. Roellinger, Oberlin College; Rebecca Ruggles, Brooklyn College.

Edwin St. Vincent, Randolph-Macon Woman's College; C. Earle Sanborn, University of Western Ontario; Stephen Sandy, Harvard University; Howard H. Schless, Columbia University; Sister Mary Thecla Schmidt, Seton Hall College; Helen M. Scurr (Bridgeport, Connecticut); Daniel Seltzer, Harvard University; Wayne Shumaker, University of California at Berkeley; Agnes Sibley, Lindenwood College; William Sloane, Dickinson College; Susan Snyder, Queens College; J. Gordon Spaulding, University of British Columbia; Albrecht B. Strauss, University of North Carolina; Richard S. Sylvester, Yale University; Wylie Sypher, Simmons College.

R. Z. Temple, Brooklyn College; Mother Thomas Aquinas, College of New Rochelle; Doris Stevens Thompson, Russell Sage College; William B. Todd, University of Texas; Cynthia J. Toussaint, Masters School; Sister Veronica Mary, Caldwell College for Women; Eugene B. Vest, University of Illinois; Sister M. Vincentia, o.p., Albertus Magnus College; Marshall Waingrow, Claremont Graduate School; Eugene M. Waith, Yale University; Andrew J. Walker, Georgia Institute of Technology; Curtis Brown Watson, Commission Franco-Américaine d'Echanges Universitaires; J. K. Welcher, St. John's University; René Wellek, Yale University; Minnie E. Wells, University of Alaska; John C. Wentz, Rutgers University; Stephen E. Whicher, Cornell University; Mother E. White, Newton College of the Sacred Heart; Brother Joseph Wiesenfarth, f.s.c., De La Salle College; Autrey Nell Wiley, Texas Woman's University; Margaret Lee Wiley, Arlington State College; Maurita Willett, University of Illinois; Edward K. Williams, DePauw University; Mother Margaret Williams, Manhattanville College of the Sacred Heart; Dorothy Willis, Adelphi College; W. K. Wimsatt, Yale University; Michael Wolff, Indiana University; Ross G. Woodman, University of Western Ontario; Samuel K. Workman, Newark College of Engineering; Nathalia Wright, University of Tennessee; Curt A. Zimansky, University of Iowa.